"Sister Funk offers the reader a helpful synthesis of the theology and practice of the Christian discernment tradition. Contemporary readers will be gently challenged to examine and reorient the way that they ha   emselves to develop 'the dis   er personal journey will   's, and students of th

                                        ....n University

"A particular value of Sr. Meg Funk's latest book is that she doesn't speak only in generalities about discernment but gives specific examples of how she and others have gone about making God-centered decisions. In addition, she provides a very helpful summary of the core teachings of classic spiritual writers like Brother Lawrence of the Resurrection and St. Teresa of Avila."

James Wiseman, OSB
The Catholic University of America
Author of *Spirituality and Mysticism:*
A Global View

Discernment Matters

Listening with the Ear of the Heart

Mary Margaret Funk, OSB

LITURGICAL PRESS

Collegeville, Minnesota

www.litpress.org

Deep gratitude to our prioress, Sister Juliann Babcock, OSB; my Benedictine community of Our Lady of Grace Monastery in Beech Grove, Indiana; and my Irish Cistercian sisters, Abbess Marie Fahy, OCSO, and nuns of St. Mary's Abbey in Glencairn, County Waterford. This set revision of the Matters Series is because of the vision and competence of Hans Christoffersen and staff at Liturgical Press, Collegeville, Minnesota.

Cover design by Jodi Hendrickson. Cover image: "Moses at the Burning Bush," by Eastern Orthodox Nun Rebecca Cown of New Skete, Cambridge, New York. Commissioned by Pamela Farris. Based on an original at the Monastery of St. Catherine, Mount Sinai, Egypt. Used by permission.

2	3	4	5	6	7	8

Library of Congress Cataloging-in-Publication Data

Funk, Mary Margaret.
    Discernment matters : listening with the ear of the heart / by Sr. Meg Funk ; preface by Rebecca Cown.
      p.   cm.
    ISBN 978-0-8146-3469-1 — ISBN 978-0-8146-3494-3 (e-book)
    1. Discernment (Christian theology)   2. Benedict, Saint, Abbot of Monte Cassino. Regula.   3. Cassian, John, ca. 360–ca. 435.   4. Spiritual life—Catholic Church.   I. Title.

BV4509.5.F86   2012
248.4'82—dc23   2012039189

To my guardian angel,
Brigid Funk,
who shows up from time to time
when discernment matters!

Contents

"Moses at the Burning Bush," by Eastern Orthodox Nun
Rebecca Cown of New Skete, Cambridge, NY,
commissioned by Pamela Farris, based on an original at
the Monastery of St. Catherine, Mount Sinai, Egypt

Iconographer's Preface

Rebecca Cown

> *By means of all created things, without exception,*
> *The Divine assails us, penetrates us, and molds us.*
> *We imagine it as distant and inaccessible.*
> *In fact, we live steeped in its burning layers.*
> —Teilhard de Chardin

One of the pillars of spiritual teaching in Eastern Christianity is deification (Greek: *theosis*),[1] which means participating or sharing in the divine nature. This is our inheritance, according to St. Dorotheus of Gaza; it is an inborn spark of divinity like a light burning deep within our hearts, within the core of our being, guiding us as we discern what pleases God, and illuminating our journey upon this earth. Christ speaks about this same light when he says we are not to hide our light under a bushel but bring it into the light of day. In this broken world, however, this inner light, this divine sensation, is often covered up by the cares and concerns of our daily lives and by our conditioning from early childhood. St. Paul also speaks about this enlightenment and the need to stay awake, to become conscious and aware—not simply about the life of our outer senses, but especially about our interior senses.[2] We call this the light of discernment. Another term is *aesthesis*, a Greek word difficult to translate into English, which we may understand as inner perception or divine sensation: a spiritual sense. Our innermost spiritual senses need to be made conscious and honed and practiced in our daily lives.

Our earliest Christian teachers reiterated that "God became human in order that the human person may become God." This divine gift presupposes our personal and collective inner work, our synergy with God. This potential has been present from the very beginning, according to the account in Genesis, since we are created in the image and likeness of God. The "image" is the reflection of God. One commentary on this Genesis passage says that "likeness" refers to being endowed with discernment and understanding. So, by inference, we might say that the "likeness" is what we are called to bring into reality by inner discernment.

St. Gregory of Nazianzus says, "Whatever is not consciously embraced cannot be transformed." That is, unless we awaken to this divine reality in our hearts, to who we really are and to what we are called, we cannot engage with this Divine Spirit within, and it will remain dormant. We are personally called to be transformed and transfigured into our God-likeness, but not just for ourselves; we are called personally to become God's agents and to enable God's ongoing creation of this world of ours.[3]

God has no other hands, feet, eyes, mind, or heart than ours to continue God's creating. The Spirit of God is everywhere present and filling all things, and human beings have been called to cocreate with God. The raw materials, so to speak, need our working with God to bring about life, harmony, peace, justice, and beauty out of chaos and disorder. God has given us the mission and purpose of incarnating God's very first words—"Let there be Light"—and to make it a living reality in our lives.

The story of Moses before the burning bush may well be a paradigm of every person's divine visitation or awakening to the divine presence. If heeded, this encounter will change a person's life. This change, or *metanoia* (Greek for "change of heart," "change of purpose, direction"), moves us away from our former identity, where the ego is in control, to become an instrument in God's hand. This is what happened to Moses, who once was a Hebrew slave, saved by an Egyptian princess. He was raised and educated as an adopted prince but later, having slain an Egyptian overseer, fled for his life into a foreign land and then became a shepherd. After many years in this lonely desert, God revealed to Moses his true identity and purpose in life.

The story tells us that Moses was tending the flock of Jethro, his father-in-law, and led the flock to the far side of the desert. He came to Horeb, the mountain of God. There, the angel of the Lord appeared to him in flames of fire from within a thorn bush. Moses saw that, although the bush was on fire, it was not consumed. So Moses thought, "I will go over and see this strange sight—why the bush is not burnt." When the Lord saw that Moses had gone over to look, God called to him from within the bush: "Moses! Moses!"

And Moses said, "Here I am."

"Do not come any closer," God said. "Take off your sandals, for the place where you are standing is holy ground." Then he said, "I am the God of your father, the God of Abraham, the God of Isaac, and the God of Jacob." At this, Moses hid his face because he was afraid to look at God.

The icon on the cover of this book depicts this encounter. Several aspects of the icon highlight our journey toward discernment. First, the bush is actually a thorn bush, typical of the desert, indicating that there isn't any place where God cannot be encountered! Next, we see the blackened sandals behind Moses. Sandals are made of the skin of animals; they are dead skins, indicating the passing nature of our persona, our identity in this world. Moses puts behind him his sense of who he has been; without it, he is vulnerable and full of fear. Yet, the icon manifests his readiness to follow the call into an unknown, to a mysterious and awesome divine encounter. His ego identity is not in control. The icon also indicates a change in his consciousness of who he really is. His clothing is radiant with divine light. His ego is not obliterated but participates in the Light of God. He has awakened to the divine spark within, to his true identity in God. His inner senses are illumined, awakened, and he hears the voice of God telling him to lead his people out of Egypt.[4]

What ensues is a dialogue with God. Moses' first reaction is "Who am I?" Stripped of his former security in who he thought he was, he now is aware of his limitations, his sense of inadequacy. But his former identity doesn't just totally disappear; for now it will become God's agent in responding to the plight of his people. God assures him, "I will be with you." To us as to Moses, this is the invitation to center our attention on a new identity—on God-consciousness, on a God who is full of compassion.

After the divine awakening comes the descent into the daily: the call for us to incarnate ("en-flesh") God's presence in this broken world. We perceive Moses' resistance, his difficulty in accepting the challenge of being God's instrument in the liberation of his people. He is *invited* by God; this mission is not forced upon him! The experience gives him the light, the strength, the discernment to face the challenges, to face his own fears, his resistances, and his limitations in fulfilling the divine mission—which is also his own purpose.

We see Moses at the foot of the holy mountain. Mount Horeb is at the bottom; the summit is Sinai, which Moses will later ascend and where he will commune with God in the deepest recesses of his being. This present encounter is his new beginning. Enlightenment is not a place where we build a tent and savor God's presence in bliss for the rest of our lives. Nevertheless, it is a divine light.

When Meg asked me to write this preface, my very first thought was a certain sense that whoever is drawn to this book has most certainly already experienced something akin to Moses' visitation (or theophany, as Eastern Christians may say). In other words, one who is drawn or deeply attracted to God must surely be responding from a God-given divine sensation, the inner light I mentioned at the beginning of this essay. Our experience may not be as dramatic as Moses' or St. Paul's experience, but even if it is more subtle, it is nonetheless real. It is one thing, however, to experience this divine presence and another to flesh it out in our lives. This process requires serious reflection on the tools for the spiritual journey. Who am I? What am I called to by God? How do I discern the path ahead? Discernment grows as we are purified in all the areas of our being.

In these times, when spiritual guides and teachers are often inaccessible, this book may well be a companion on the journey, one that will support us through what may feel like a labyrinth or a maze as we make our way through the complexities of everyday life and the seasons of more profound changes. Just as Moses in the desert received what he needed to discern his new life, these writings by Meg Funk offer tools for growth in self-knowledge, for deepening our relationship to God, and for growing in discernment with God-consciousness in our own life and purpose.

Rebecca Cown
New Skete
Cambridge, New York

Introduction

We desire God. In our hearts we feel this longing. Discernment is finding that still, small, "as if" voice of God. This seeking is inner work. We have sound teachings from the monastic tradition to help us. Through our spiritual senses, the ear of our heart actually awakens.

This way of living is a personal relationship with God. We make choices to go this direction of our heart's desire. Making these decisions through the help of the Holy Spirit is discernment. We are not alone. We are free to make choices on our own, but in faith we have a warm invitation to welcome accompaniment by the Holy Spirit. This is discernment: to sort our thoughts and follow the impulse of grace given by the Holy Spirit. Since we are not our thoughts, we can observe them rising and follow the ones that are from God. We learn to listen to the voice of the Holy Spirit rather than our own voice, self talking to the self. The voice of the Holy Spirit is a dynamic voice that we hear and heed through our interior senses. This voice gives directives for action. Then, as promised by Christ, we can act confidently. This Christ alive in us points us to our Abba/Father and brings the reign of God into our very fractured world.

This book was difficult to write as it presumes that the reader is familiar with the previous four books, both in theory and in practice.[1] Readers of the previous books might find this text to be repetitious, but the advantage of this work is another opportunity for me to share these teachings after years of dialogue with other souls so blessed by grace on this spiritual journey. What is the story of the Matters Series?

First, when I was prioress and gave conferences on the Rule of Benedict to the nuns at Beech Grove, Indiana, I discovered John Cassian and his masterpiece of literature about the eight thoughts. Hence, *Thoughts Matter* (1998). When I was teaching and giving retreats at Benedict Inn, student questions put me back to the research to find the antidotes to the afflictions. Hence, *Tools Matter* (2001). When I was coordinating programs for Monastic Interreligious Dialogue, I found the uniquely kenotic spirituality of Christianity. Hence, *Humility Matters* (2006). When I was engaged in doing *lectio divina*, I discovered the early desert tradition that emphasized the spiritual senses. I wrote the book, *Lectio Matters* (2010). Now, after fifty years of my own experience of being a nun as well as living in Ireland, I have been invited to listen with the ear of my heart to the Holy Spirit. Hence, *Discernment Matters* (2013).

While the Matters Series was a slow immersion into the theory and practice of the monastic way of life, I tell the story of my own conversion in the Bolivian event of

1984. Hence, *Into the Depths* (2011). *Discernment Matters* is, then, the most comprehensive presentation of why this inner work is not only necessary but also such a joy.

This book is a source for those who want to learn and practice discernment as taught by the early monastic tradition. First, I present a short summary of the teachings about discernment from monastic traditions of late antiquity (second through eighth centuries). Then, to make discernment practical, I include decisions that need to be made today. I share examples of monastics using discernment for selecting books for *lectio*, the practice of the cell, and wearing the habit. I offer three examples of programs that teach discernment, such as a one-hundred-day retreat, selfless service opportunities, a pilgrimage, and seasonal visitation to an elder. Finally, I lift up two examples of saints who embodied discernment: St. Benedict, who taught moderation, and St. Patrick, who infused a Christ consciousness in Ireland.

While the monastic way of life is designed to give form to discernment as a way of life, lay contemplatives can adapt these teachings to suit. We ask God's blessing on this important work. There's no better time to start than now. What is discernment? How do we know that we are doing it?

Introductory Teaching on Discernment

When Jesus of Nazareth prepared his followers for his departure, he was careful not to leave them orphans

(John 14:15-21). He spoke warmly and without commentary, using a direct approach that there was One to come after him who would be with them in an abiding manner. He introduced them to this Person, whom he called the Holy Spirit. This Spirit would help each individual and the group as a whole. Jesus said that he must leave because if he did not depart and return to his Abba/Father, the Spirit would not come. This Spirit would bring to their minds all that Jesus taught; would defend in times of persecution, trial, and temptation; would quicken their minds, anoint their bodies, and warm their souls. Christ Jesus breathed this Spirit into his disciples. It has never been seen by physical eyes but has been felt and known by all who have looked into their hearts with the eyes of their soul. This Spirit has many names, but the work of this Spirit is discernment. It sanctifies and enjoins us all into communion, not in some other realm, but in this household of Earth. This Person is as distinct as Jesus the Christ. This Person, the Holy Spirit, is the soul of our soul. This Spirit shows us that the entry to this way of life is following the Gospel, that Good News brought to us by Jesus' life and death and resurrection.

The work of the Christian way of life is not a mechanical membership in a church as an institution but participation with one's own experience of God through an interior life. The secular culture provides a world of self-consciousness, which is a healthy expression of autonomy. We have a separate soul and a distinctiveness as a person created by God that is never to be annihilated.

But we seek immersion into a God consciousness. When we are young children we seem to have this God consciousness, but it is soon forgotten. We can recover this childlike immediacy with God through a combination of doing good works in our exterior life and noticing our thoughts in our interior life. We are not our thoughts. The thoughts can be sorted out, and we can follow the thoughts that remove confusion, compulsion, and forgetfulness. This work of sorting our thoughts is discernment. We can learn to listen with the ear of our hearts because we stand in place before the Living God. Like Moses, we take off our shoes. In real life, we walk in the Presence with our feet grounded in our daily rounds of work and prayer. We make choices that transform our self-centered habits toward dynamic love of others. God's reign has already started and we are a part of this dynamism. We have a limited capacity to sustain this noble work, but with the help of the Holy Spirit we can do this with joy and equanimity. A source for these teachings on discernment can be found in the literature of the early monastic tradition.

Finding This Tradition:
The Sources in the Rule of St. Benedict

As I shared in the story of how the Matter Series was written it was when I was prioress that I started giving conferences on the Rule of Benedict. I taught this sixth-century text using my training in Scripture. I followed the footnotes and sources that Benedict (b. 480) quoted in his teachings. The Rule is short: only a prologue and seventy-three chapters, about 850 verses. Benedict quotes Scripture 324 times, either directly or as an allusion. He also quotes thirty-four ancient and patristic sources. His most frequently cited teacher is John Cassian (146 quotes). This was a discovery for me as I had been a Benedictine nun for twenty-five years and had never read John Cassian. In the 1980s there was not a contemporary English translation of Cassian's *Institutes* and *Conferences*, even though in chapter 73 Benedict instructs his followers to follow the directives of the *Institutes* and their *Lives* (RB 73.5). I read and studied an old translation of Cassian; then I followed the sources of Cassian's teachers and found that his favorite teacher was Evagrius. I studied Evagrius and found that his dominant teacher was Origen, of the Alexandrian school of exegesis. While Christ Jesus is our only teacher, I had discovered a lineage that provided me, through the Rule of Benedict, a direct line of transmission. I belonged to and was vowed in a living tradition through the Benedictine way of life.

What was more exciting than being in a sturdy lineage of the monastic tradition was that the actual teachings were accessible to me through recent English translations of this literature. After some years of study and prayerful *lectio* I was quite taken with the theme and directives on discernment. In the writings of late antiquity (from the second to the eighth centuries), almost 30 percent of the teachings from this early monastic history are on the topic of discernment. No other concern caused more interaction between the abbot and the monastic or the elder and the novice. Having found my tradition through the Scriptures, the Rule of Benedict, and his sources, I have tried to provide a short catechesis in this book, *Discernment Matters*. With all that preparation, then, what is discernment?

A Working Definition of Discernment

Discernment is following the inclination of grace, those personal, subtle promptings of the Holy Spirit. Decisions become sacraments of grace when we yield to "Your will be done, on earth as it is in heaven" (Matt 6:10). We need the Holy Spirit to nourish us with this kind of daily bread, this living relationship that guides and perfects what has begun in us through Christ. We need deliverance from self seeking self, from dominant cultural conditioning, and from influences of evil. For our part, we stand ready to forgive and ask to refrain from all the causes and conditions that compromise our heart's desire, which is God. Discernment is our relationship with the Holy Spirit who is at work in us. We (the Holy Spirit and us with our heart's longing) are in this loving relationship together.

A Teaching on the Holy Spirit That Matters

About ten years ago, having been a nun for forty years, I noticed that I'd follow the liturgical cycle from Advent,

Christmas, Epiphany, Lent, Holy Week, and Easter year after year. During Ordinary Time (thirty-four weeks), I'd linger with the Christ who was subtly present to his disciples before he ascended to heaven. My piety and devotion were walking and abiding with the Christ who appeared to his disciples as a teacher in faith. I never tired of the post-Easter narratives: Mary meeting our Lord in the garden, the Emmaus story of the breaking of the bread and recognizing Jesus, and Jesus cooking breakfast for his fishing disciples. This Christ was very close and so intimate that the years simply followed one after another.

Pentecost would come, I would participate in the liturgical year as a matter of routine, but then I would go back to my postresurrection consciousness of Jesus being present to his disciples during those forty days between the resurrection and ascension.

This, I thought, was good enough for me: I felt that Jesus was very present, he was very alive and well in my life, and I loved those gospel stories. But gradually I realized that I never went beyond the ascension and, consequently, I never entered into Pentecost.

So I think it was an invitation by the Holy Spirit that I did my habitual, sustained *lectio divina*, but this time on the theme of Pentecost.[2] I took this passage from the Acts of the Apostles, the coming of the Holy Spirit:

> When the day of Pentecost had come, they were all together in one place. And suddenly from heaven there

came a sound like the rush of a violent wind, and it filled the entire house where they were sitting. Divided tongues, as of fire, appeared among them, and a tongue rested on each of them. All of them were filled with the Holy Spirit and began to speak in other languages, as the Spirit gave them ability. (Acts 2:1-4)

This passage of only four verses is the famous source in the whole of the Bible that is considered to name the feast of Pentecost as the birth of the church. So I took up the sustained method of *lectio divina*, using the four voices of the text received by my four senses.[3]

First, I did a thorough exegesis of that passage, those four verses from the second chapter of Acts. I followed up on every footnote, every allusion that took me back into the Old Testament with the whole prophetic tradition. I asked, "What was Pentecost?" Pentecost was a confluence of three feast days:

1. One feast was when Moses received the law and after fifty days handed the Law of Salvation to the people. The law was read to them, and they said, "All that you have said, we will do." So it's that remembrance of consenting to the law of Moses that became the feast of Pentecost.

2. Another feast was held by the Hebrew people fifty days after the Passover to celebrate being saved from slavery and entering into the Promised Land. The Hebrew people became the People of Israel.

3. The third tradition was an agricultural feast day opening the harvest celebration: sacrifice of firstfruits and festival time for a people faithful to the law of Moses.

It was revealing that I did not know the roots of Pentecost, though I had done my Old Testament studies as part of my academic work. The early church borrowed from the Hebrew calendar, and it merged these three feasts with the fifty days after Jesus rose from the dead.

After exploring the origins of the feast, I went back to the Old Testament and reread and studied the prophetic texts, including Exodus 13, Isaiah 66, and Joel, listed in the footnotes. Jesus was the fulfillment of the promise; he was the Messiah who was named in the Old Testament as the fulfillment of Israel in all its connectivity and also for us individually. Jesus is the presence of God in each one of our hearts.

So the Old Testament study was informative, but then I went forward to the New Testament and pursued all the answers to these questions: What was the reign of God? What was the *kerygma*, the Good News?

I reread the four gospels, which share the narrative stories of Jesus himself. Then I read the Acts of the Apostles and the letters. The apostles continued being historical witnesses of Christ's teachings.

I continued my study and meditation into the *Life of St. Anthony*, which was written by Athanasius, as he had all the indicators of being a prophet. I saw how the new genre of hagiography (in 357 CE) read back into the prophetic literature and brought it forward onto Anthony to make the point that he was the prophet that now extended Christ into the New Covenant. Athanasius himself writes his own destiny into the script by using language of Elijah giving the spirit of double proportion to Elisha and leaving the cloak or mantle. We are told that Anthony is the new Elijah and Athanasius is the new Elisha.

Then, I found the same motif in Gregory the Great's book 2 of *The Dialogues*. St. Benedict's story is also told in hagiographical form. Twenty of the almost forty chapters are allusions to either Elijah or Elisha, both from the books of Kings.

So as we study the prophetic passages describing the entrance of the Holy Spirit in the New Testament, we see that each one of us who has been baptized in the Spirit shares this charismatic tradition. Jesus said, "If in my name you ask me for anything, I will do it" (John 14:14).[4]

The study of the Scriptures is essential to understanding, but I also read several books about the Holy Spirit, the prophetic tradition, and the reign of God. In that study I asked these questions: Was the Holy Spirit a cosmic Christ? Was the Holy Spirit the spirit of Jesus that is in us, like the Jesus who has left earthly life? Was the Holy Spirit just undifferentiated mystery and all matter? Is the Spirit a distinct person toward whom my heart would be praying? Are we to feel the presence of the Holy Spirit as distinct from the Father and the Son?[5]

In the study phase of *lectio* on Pentecost, I confirmed that the Holy Spirit is real and has a relational ontic identity without entity. The Holy Spirit is a person. This Spirit is someone we can count on, we can pray to, we can invoke. This personal experience of indwelling has the feeling of immersion in oxygen, like a realm of cosmic energy. Presence is never not everywhere; we learn to apprehend it quicker and with more depth of knowing. Dynamic, real, actual grace seems new and now.

When we go to Mass every day here at the monastery, the priest lays his hands over the elements on the altar and calls down the Holy Spirit, that these elements— this bread, this wine—will become the Body and Blood of Christ. This moment is called the *epiclesis*. The priest invokes the Holy Spirit to effect that dynamic energy and to sanctify those elements.

And then later in the Mass the priest prays another *epiclesis*: that we who have partaken of this food become the body and blood of Christ as a group and as individuals. So there are two invocations—*epicleses*—of the Holy Spirit. And as the bread and wine become the Body and Blood of our Lord Jesus Christ, so too may we partake of this sacrament and become Christ for others.

Though I'd known about the Holy Spirit, I felt no devotion to this Person. I could not identify with a number, the Third Person of the Blessed Trinity, nor with an image of a dove or a legal advocate called Paraclete. This abstract conceptual notion has changed irrevocably in the last few years. Gradually, the Spirit came more and more into my consciousness. I know other Christians report a sudden infusion. This is not my experience. The shift from a devotion to our Lord to a devotion to the Holy Spirit was personal and intimate; it felt like a call to a deeper interior life of mystery. We call this Person "Sophia," "Advocate," "Sanctifier," or "Holy Spirit." There are all kinds of names and words for this coming of Divine Uncreated Energy, but no name can aptly describe this Presence. The Holy Spirit is presence coming from within. It is an inner experience for me. The face of God is found in Jesus Christ. We can see God, as Jesus said that anyone who sees him sees the Father. The Holy Spirit is known by my spiritual senses, not the eyes of my face. There's no devotion to the Holy Spirit that is freestanding and apart from Christ who takes us to the Abba/Father. The Trinity is not an abstract principle but concrete reality. We know God because of Jesus, and the Spirit of Jesus links us to the Mystery of the Trinity. I am related to the Trinity in my own human person.[6]

I could identify with Pentecost being a formative event for the disciples gathered in one place. In the Old Testament, "one place," a place of God, is code for having the experience of God's presence. For me, this gradual awakening was neither dramatic nor anything I shared with others. I've heard many other contemplatives speak of this happening to them too. The event, the story of Pentecost, is actual. I have learned from my experience that Pentecost happens to us as individuals and also as a community. Pentecost is the birth of the church.

After some weeks of study about the literal text of Pentecost, I was drawn to understand the *meaning* of

Pentecost and then the urgency of how the Holy Spirit wants to be active in my life. The Holy Spirit comes and enlightens my judgment, gives me answers, gives me insights, gives me the way to go. I feel, when I call for help, that the Holy Spirit enkindles my heart and fills my mind with the right thoughts, wisdom, understanding, compassion, and fear of the Lord. I gradually began to ask the Holy Spirit about everything that was on my heart. Should I do this, say that, or accompany that person? Should I continue this work, start another, or be ready to let go of this project or that work in progress? Discernment replaced the day-to-day decisions that I formerly did for myself—consulting myself and doing my best, after some inner chatter, with a wink and a prayer.

I began to count on this gift of the Holy Spirit in my daily life. This was when I understood that the Holy Spirit is real. I called on the Holy Spirit and felt the courage to act with an inner strength that was sturdy and abiding. I felt for the first time that I was coming out of another domain, not my ego, not even my preferences; I was coming out of another place where there were confirming signs that these decisions were coming from God and not from my usual ego-driven self. There were fruits of the Holy Spirit that came from my actions, but I had nothing to do with them. I also had a felt realization that, even though the Spirit is distinct from Jesus, there was no shift in my relationship with Jesus that was away from our usual patterns. The Holy Spirit dimension was a natural progression into love for our Lord. Another part of the dynamic was that there was no possible way to slip into a "Jesus and me" cult or a "Holy Spirit and Meg" cozy nest. This energy was radically plural and outward bound. Prayer is never private but always personal and universally engaged. I'm not sure any of my sisters noticed it, but I had no fear about losing my balance or going to some extreme spirituality. From the inside I felt poised and compassionate.

So, in rereading these four lines from the Acts of the Apostles I felt my own transmission into this Holy Spirit who actually came and was at work in me. Discernment is the work we did together. This Spirit came and I listened with the ear of my heart. This *lectio* lasted for ten months, from the Ascension in May to the following Ash Wednesday in February.

This first period of zeal and fervor did not last. It faded when I got busy and moved my mind's eye to task after task instead of this inner work. Listening with the ear of the heart, which is the Pentecost agenda, shifted back up into my head. I was soon talking to myself again. I was listening to my self talking to self. I was at risk of returning to my former way of life rather than hearing the impulse of grace. I needed training in discernment.

I entered a monastery to do this inner work, and while from time to time I've given attention to my inner life, for the most part I've been an active administrator, teacher, and community worker. It took me twenty-five years to know the Rule of Benedict and its sources and another twenty-five to learn discernment. I've been a nun for

3/26/14 Let's turn - to learn discernment

fifty years here at Our Lady of Grace Monastery in Beech Grove, Indiana, and have a fine education and live with holy nuns, but it seems to me that I am a beginner learning how to discern, which is a particular kind of listening. I had found this living God, but I faded from the theater like an actor darting off stage. I returned to my former way of life of being okay but not very connected during prayers, during common observances, or even during times alone in my cell.

After a few failed attempts at trying to find a place for training, a teacher, or a group of like-minded souls, it became clear that we do not need one more institution, one more foundation, one more abbey or monastery, or one more social network. I knew the teachings on discernment, but I needed to do them as a habit, not just from time to time. My own practice and *praxis* are what matter. Discernment is living into the relationship with the Holy Spirit impelling me toward God. Hence, the title of this book: *Discernment Matters*.

Wisdom from the Early Monastic Tradition

Tradition teaches that all of us have this inner work to do because we have inner tendencies to act from self-centeredness rather than from God-centeredness. We are burdened with afflictions. According to early monastic sources, there are eight afflictions that pertain to food, sex, things, anger, dejection, *acedia*, vainglory, and pride. Training in practice is helpful to root out these habits. Afflictions are replaced with ceaseless prayer. The main practice is sustained *lectio divina*, which, when done in a sustained manner, leads us into discernment as a way of life.

We have already seen how influential the Rule of St. Benedict is in bringing forward the teachings on this inner life. We know that he assumes his followers are familiar with the writings of John Cassian, who wrote the theory and practice of religious life. Cassian's *Institutes* and *Conferences* include hefty teachings on the topic of discernment.[7]

Begin with Prayer

St. Benedict says that whenever we begin anything, we must begin with earnest prayer and beg God with our prayer to bring it to completion (RB Prol. 4). As we know from Scripture, the Spirit hovered over the waters during creation and overshadowed the events in the New Testament: Jesus' baptism, the transfiguration, Mary's annunciation, and Pentecost. In discernment, we place ourselves under this Spirit that is hovering. We ask for no less than the same shaft of divine energy for our souls.

As we want to be quickened in our decisions, we linger here and invoke the Holy Spirit to come, inspire, dwell, abide, and let not fear or anxiety hinder our deliberations. We can simply rely on the Holy Spirit to bring to mind what needs to be done, when, where, how, and why. We do not know what is best, but God does. The Holy Spirit is the plan.

Chapter 1

Discernment and the Holy Spirit

M y intention here is not so much to consider *how* discernment works but *that* it works and that we can be certain of this relationship with Christ, with and in the Holy Spirit. The head understands when it is a felt experience, but language struggles to describe this inner way of knowing. Following the gospels, we imitate Christ. He soon becomes our consciousness. We have our own experience of Christ's life, death, resurrection, our own immersion into the paschal mystery. The event reported in the Acts of the Apostles—Pentecost—actually happens to each of us to some degree. We feel the presence of the Spirit. The Holy Spirit wants to be involved in our lives, year by year, day by day, and moment by moment. Enjoying this abiding Spirit dwelling in us and among us is possible in this lifetime.[1]

[handwritten margin note: (8) afflictions: food, sex, things, anger, dejection, acedia, vainglory, pride]

The factors that prevent us from having a direct experience of the Holy Spirit are our afflictions. These afflictions can be rooted out from our body, mind, and soul. When the afflictions are extirpated, we abide in peace. We want the whole of our life to be toward God and so we invoke the Holy Spirit often, and this Spirit comes not only in faith but also in actual moment-by-moment decisions of daily life. There can be decision making by an individual or a group, but there's no discernment without the Holy Spirit.

The word "discernment" comes from the Greek word *diakrisis*, which means "to sort."[2] A factor that must be considered is the impulse or grace of the Spirit. Sometimes we decide to go from here to there or to do this or that. We see our choices and take action. Without training in discernment, there is a tendency to ignore the Holy Spirit who wants to be consulted, to make known what is the good to be done, the best option. This Spirit never overrides my free will, my conscience, or my individual spirit that was created in God's image and likeness, but this Spirit is available to my mind. I've learned that I need to invite the Third Person of the Holy Trinity into my deliberations if I want to avoid my default: thinking mind talking to myself. This collaboration with the Holy Spirit, rather than independent self-talk, is discernment. I refrain from self talking to the self and lean into discernment. What is God's way for me? I pray and then sort my thoughts.

[handwritten margin note: pray, wait, patience, ponder, 24 hrs, observe]

This training in the practice of discernment has been tested and treasured in the monastic tradition. While it may seem ponderous, these teachings are valuable to

[handwritten note at bottom: patience, persistence, perseverance]

learn how to listen to the Holy Spirit. When we listen, we hear thoughts, feelings, emotions. This inner chatter comes quickly, frequently, and loudly, but there are skillful ways of managing our thoughts. If we pause, back out of our thinking mind for a moment, and observe, we can use all these packets of internal data. We begin our sorting, our discernment. This training is about listening with the ear of our hearts. This is a big shift away from thinking that goes up the chain of content, rather than observing the endless flood of thoughts that come and that go.

Thoughts and Prayer

In this book, we will attend to the classic instruction about our thoughts—our inner thoughts that lead us either to virtue or to vice—and then we will look at the teachings on prayer that can help us prevent our thoughts from rising or help us overcome them if they are leading us astray.

The thoughts can cause a relapse and can trick us into acting the way we did before we entered the monastery, but the antidote is to begin a strenuous effort toward a sustained practice of rooting out vices (habitual faults) and replacing them with virtues (habitual compassion). This is the ascetical life of a spiritual athlete. We literally go into interior training of the mind, and the afflictions are a port of entry. This is the combat that takes place in one's mind and heart.

When I first engaged in this interior work, I underestimated the effort entailed. I didn't take up the edges that words like "combat" and "athlete" connote. I thought that violence begets violence so those military words were not necessary. Now, almost thirty years later, I smile at my naïveté. While "the fight" needs to be done with gentle confidence and steady resolve, the intensity of the battle certainly is like a sustained war. The trick is to be focused and ready like a warrior or a world-class athlete but at the same time to be meek and docile like a faun at daybreak.

We need a method of discernment. We observe and notice all that rises on the screen of consciousness. The traditional word for this sorting is "discernment." We sort our thoughts of food, sex, things, anger, dejection, *acedia*, vainglory, and pride.

This sorting is not analytic speculation but the hard work of directing our own thoughts that rise in our minds. Again, we are not alone. We have the Holy Spirit, and we also have tradition that gives us sturdy instruction. We are not our thoughts (and feelings), but thoughts can be a skillful means to find our heart.

The teachings on the thoughts are the heart of discernment. We can sort our thoughts according to content, as in the list of the eight deadly thoughts given above. We can also sort our thoughts by seeing the stage of their rising and clustering into an entity with energy and action. We can sort our thoughts by looking at their sources, their directions, and their "spirits." We can also sort our thoughts according to frequency and persistence.

The ways of sorting constitute the theory behind discernment. Yet, an important fact to notice about the practice of discernment is watching, noticing, and observing, not thinking, as in analysis and examination.

The problem with using the thinking mind is twofold. First, we see that our thoughts are contaminated. Debris from the human condition prevents the mind from reporting as clearly as a mirror. Our logical thinking mind cannot leap out of the loop, but our intuitive mind can step back and watch. Second, the logical mind usually misses the symbolic voice heard by the intuitive senses. But, most of all, discernment is an opportunity to hear the moral sense with one's personal senses. This is the place of the heart. We listen with the ear of our heart and respond by repenting, rooting out our tendencies toward personal sin, and replacing those habitual thoughts with ceaseless prayer.

Method
listen
respond
replace

The Afflictive Thought: Thoughts in General

The theory about the afflictions in the spiritual life owes its root teachings to the Greek idea of body, mind, and soul (spirit). The Holy Spirit is seen as the soul of the soul for the Christian thinkers from the School of Alexandria.[3]

The insight that thoughts come and thoughts go gave rise to a priority of the moral life. We can direct our thoughts, and if we do not entertain them, then they leave the mind undisturbed. The mind can contemplate, rest on, direct, or get involved with these passing thoughts. When one removes, stills, or orders the thoughts, there is a pervading stillness, a peace, an equanimity that prevails.

So it is a worthwhile goal to attend to our thoughts and root out the ones that are not of God.

The fact that we are not our thoughts gives rise to the whole interior journey being one of active and passive work. There's inner work to do and it is difficult, but it is not impossible. We can use these thoughts or be used by them.

There's a chain of thoughts. Thoughts "thought about" become desires, desires become passions, beneficial thoughts become virtues, and destructive thoughts become vices.

There are more than these eight afflictive thoughts—food, sex, things, anger, dejection, *acedia*, vainglory, and pride—but these are classic, meaning they occur in all of us, through all times and in all cultures and in every generation. We might not have each of them, but the potential for them is present and we know it when we see it in ourselves or in others. Though we have thoughts, we are not our thoughts. We can direct them, which is called discernment.

The sources of the thoughts can come from ourselves, from God, from others, or from evil forces, even an entity we call the Evil One. The sources usually indicate the kinds of thoughts—good, bad, and indifferent—since if they are sourced in good, they usually go toward good, or if they are sourced in evil, they usually go toward evil. Second thoughts are important to notice. Our intentions matter too. Second thoughts become intentions or motivations. Motivations govern indifferent thoughts toward good or evil and can influence even the most heroic thoughts and actions to return us to selfish gains and vainglorious results.

Tradition has it that evil can influence thoughts from the outside but cannot touch one's soul unless there's consent. We are under the reign of God and nothing can ultimately harm us. Though our thoughts cycle over and over again, we become more skillful at recognizing them. This is the art and practice of discernment. Thoughts can consolidate into stubborn afflictions or even compulsions that harden into addictions, but there's always a way out. This is the training in discernment.

Some of us have a greater percentage of agency (freedom) to direct, distinguish, and determine our thoughts. Every person is born with inherent biochemicals that lead to compulsivity, yet some people have so little freedom from this compulsivity that, through no fault of their own, there's a small window of freedom to make choices. This human condition factor is why thoughts matter. No matter how little is the discretion, this area of freedom is our part in the work of right effort to do good and avoid evil.

The Afflictive Thought: A Starting Place for Discernment

The sequence of the eight afflictions is logical and may not be one's particular story. An affliction is an adversity, but it can also be in service of the spiritual life. There is a gift when we transcend each affliction. When we pass through one of the afflictions, we can look back and see the benefit, the fruits that emerge on the other side. When afflictions subside, Christ consciousness rises!

There is one overall indicator that thoughts need modulating with quick attention before they create danger for the soul: "Extremes meet," say the ancient monks. It's equally adverse to have too little as too much of a thing.[4]

The most compelling reason why thoughts matter is that when we let our mind go into free-fall mindlessness, listlessness, or laziness, our casual unbidden thoughts become our consciousness: food consciousness, sex consciousness, thing consciousness, etc. The goal is Christ consciousness—an abiding consciousness of God's presence. The teachings on the eight thoughts are not to cause discouragement but to help us identify our difficulties and learn the tools to root out and even prevent these thoughts from becoming afflictions. The Holy Spirit is our guide. The work is discernment.

Anatomy of a Thought

Let's review again the anatomy of a thought and how it starts and gains strength and sways us into action. This list is helpful because if we can catch our thoughts early, often, and as gently as possible, we will be able to refrain from the energies of the afflictions that cloud our discrimination. This is the first stage of discernment: sorting our thoughts, watching them rise, and noticing that we are not our thoughts.

Elders differentiated between moments of temptation. The suggestion in thought (*prosbole*) is free from blame (*anaitios*). Next follows the coupling (*syndiasmos*), an inner dialogue with the suggestion of and struggle against a temptation, which may end with victory or with consent (*synkatathesis*). Such consent is the actual sin. When repeated, such acts produce a passion (*pathos*) and, in the end, a terrible captivity of the soul (*aichmalosia*) that is no longer able to withstand the force of the Evil One.

> The proper object of *exagoreusis ton logismon* (revelation of thoughts) is the first stage of this process, the *prosbole*. One must crush the serpent's head as soon as it appears. . . . All this is done through an entire strategy: *nepsis* (vigilance), watchfulness, the guarding of the heart (*custodia cordis*) and of the mind, prayer, especially the invocation of the name of Jesus, and so forth.[5]

In *The Ladder of Divine Assent*, John Climacus includes teachings on how thoughts come and go. Here, he reports the distinctions hallowed before his time (579–649 CE).[6]

Thoughts go from:

1. provocation (thoughts rise, simply rise)
2. coupling with dialogue (an interactive phase)
3. assent (moving along the possibility)
4. captivity (got attention toward doing it)
5. struggle and consent (*pathos*)
6. passion (the full disease/pattern: captivity)

Thoughts have an anatomy from beginning to end. When seekers would go to a desert elder, they attended to the movements of the heart (of the mind), suggestions, inner promptings. When such an impulse or inner prompting developed into an outward deed, into consent that eventually became habitual, it would be too late to show all this to the director. Confession, as in the sacrament of reconciliation, is a more appropriate forum to seek absolution from end-stage thoughts that have become sin. But to prevent thoughts from going into full-blown patterns of sin, it is beneficial to go to a wise elder and manifest our thoughts and urges.

Manifestation of thoughts gives us the opportunity for honesty and truth bearing; it can help us notice when we get hooked and take action that is against our best self. This also helps us to notice the content of the thought (for example, food, sex, things, etc.) and the stage of the thought, the consent, the patterns of *pathos*.

I want to linger here to point out the importance of the teaching of the thoughts (*logismois*). We soon find that it is not the content of the thought that is most troublesome; it is the stage of the thought itself. It is like a virus that is infectious. The strain, as to the particular kind, might vary in degree of toxicity, but what is most important is to stop the chain of the thought from thickening into an entity that cannot be backed down from having a life of its own. Maybe the analogy of cancer is appropriate here. All cancer is to be avoided, and the earlier the treatment, the better the prognosis of being free from the destructive nature of the disease. Here is another look at the stages:

- A thought rises.

- An image appears.

- The dialogue of my mind is accompanied by an image,

- which ends in invitation to (a) continue the dialogue or (b) refrain from the same.

- I consent to the inner promptings of further imaging and conversation inside my head, accompanied by feelings.

- The thought gets solid with entity and offers a suggestion to take action.

- I either take action or refrain from the invitation or temptation.

- There's a simultaneous melody line that is another conversation with the thought and the person in this thinking mode about intention or motivation; tradition calls this the "second thought."

- I act on the invitation one time.

- I continue in that direction of the original prompting (an affliction).

- I continue being engaged with that thought that is now an entity with emotion (passion).

- I act often in collaboration with the entity, and it becomes a habit (pattern).

- I then dwell in that ethos of suffering (*pathos*) until

- this entity becomes my identity (captivity).

- I am the thought! I start acting as if this thought is me—possessed by illusion.

Repetition and Intensity

Discernment not only sorts the content of the thought, the stage of the thought, and the source and goal of the thought but also notices the repetition of that same thought rising from underneath consciousness over and over again. This sequence can be mesmerizing and almost hypnotic and, with repetition over time, can be obsessive. The teaching is to remember that we are not our thoughts, no matter how often they recur. We stay awake and watch.

The theory is that our thoughts loop around and hook us. We can watch our thoughts (*nepis*) and see the points of contact, invitation, and consent of the will. Some thoughts are slicker and more insidious and catch us before we catch them. We need help.

The work of our interior life is discernment. We discern our thoughts. These thoughts rise first as an inclination and then as an image with a story connecting the inclination to our feelings or desires. Next comes an invitation to act on the desire. This act, at first, is a single moment of enjoyment but can become a habit with repeated fulfillment of the desire, whether in mind or physically in behavior. If this habit is done for some time and affirmed by the intellect, this can soon become stitched together with our innermost identity. The reason thoughts matter so much is that this rising of a thought is where we can discern where, what, who, and how God is acting in our lives.

Eight Afflictive Thoughts[7]

These afflictive thoughts are classic. They seem to be ever present in each generation and all peoples. No one has all of them, but the theory of how they progress is helpful to each of us. Because the afflictions are a starting point for discernment to clear the mind so that I can hear the Holy Spirit, I am providing a comprehensive list for self-examination.

I've experienced my own nothingness and have had my own experience of the Holy Spirit. I realize that these chronic negative thoughts are separating me from consciousness of an abiding sense of God's presence.

When our minds are still and at peace, we can hear that subtle whisper of grace and take action accordingly. But most of the time we are covered over with one of the afflictive consciousnesses of food, sex, things, anger, dejection, *acedia*, vainglory, or pride. Our right effort is to refrain from these inclinations, and then the Spirit takes over, giving us the impulse of grace needed to cultivate virtue.

Isn't there an easier way, we might ask? There's always the possibility of total, sudden, and quick transformation.

God's grace abounds, but in the monastic tradition this ascetical work with the thoughts seems to be the usual and even preferred way to encounter that grace. Through the low door of humility, we admit our weakness and cry for help, which comes in the person of the Holy Spirit.

First Affliction of the Body: Thoughts of Food

The food thought is a good starting point to perceive that you have thoughts and to observe them. It is also the beginning of training for prayer because food is a tool for connecting with people and nature and for expressing our relationship with God. Our bodies need food for well-being and health. This physical vitality is also beneficial in providing endurance in our spiritual lives. The training is not about the food or drink but rather about noticing and working with the thought of food.

Our bodies give us signals about hunger and thirst. The first step in discriminating is to "sort" our thoughts about these signals. This sorting is called *diakrisis*, and the food thoughts are usually about when to eat (time and frequency), the refinement of the food (quality), and how much to eat (quantity). The training of the mind at this discernment stage is fasting using the "middle way" to check these four decision points about what kind of food, when, how often, and how much. Fasting is a natural way to notice these thoughts because it is easy to sense hunger.

Fasting is eating mindfully with full attention, and it moderates the food thought. In contrast, gluttony is indiscriminate eating or drinking. When we no longer have freedom to make choices that direct our food management, we give in to our impulses. It is risky to be on the edges, the extremes. When one shifts too far in one direction, it is an indication that one's food thoughts are out of balance or even out of control. Too little food is as objectionable and against the training as too much; too poor in quality is as bad as too rich; too infrequent is as harmful as overeating. Once we get our lives in order in relation to the food thought, the tendency is to evaluate another's correct amount of food or drink. In the Christian tradition, the dominant scriptural mandate is "charity prevails." Refrain from judging the motives and behaviors of another. What is too much for one may not be enough for another.

There are two exceptions to fasting: feast days and hospitality. We do not fast when it is time to celebrate the graciousness of God's gifts to us. On feast days we are encouraged to eat something special, more often, and in a little more quantity. In hospitality we lay aside our middle-way patterns by serving the guest first. This discernment is using the other's needs rather than our own as the criteria of eating and drinking. The guest is God.

To abstain consistently from certain foods or drink is a worthy practice. For example, observant Muslims, Buddhists, and Hindus may refrain from all alcohol, and Muslims and Jews do not eat pork. This abstaining is not about prohibiting certain foods or drinks so much as it is about using these options as an object of training, just as an athlete uses resistance tools to strengthen muscles and bones. Similarly, in the Hindu tradition certain foods, such as meat, garlic, radishes, and onions, are considered intrinsically harmful to the interior life. In contrast, foods that are subtler in vibration are helpful to stilling the mind. It is important to remember, however, that these particular practices belong to their traditions. As Christians all foods are good and holy unless they give scandal or have been offered to idols in sacrifice. A few days are set aside for the discipline of abstaining from meat during Lent.

There is one thought about food that is transformative: why is one eating or drinking? Fasting helps me know my thoughts and keeps me supple enough to hear the grace moving through my heart. Food is only a tool for my relationship with God. The food thought can dominate my consciousness, which would be a barrier to my deeper stillness and predisposition toward prayer. A fruit of the contemplative life is the joy of eating mindfully with praise and gratitude. The food thought is entry-level training of the mind for discernment.

Second Affliction of the Body: Thoughts of Sex

The second thought is about sex. The sex thought is like food insofar as it is the body's hunger, but sex is the desire for physical enjoyment of another's body. Sexual desire is a universal experience that has immense, persistent power from puberty until death. There is no question about the goodness, health, and wholeness, as well as holiness, that sexual energies serve. Nevertheless, if not well ordered, sexual passions can also destroy and actually deny us life. No one is called to suppress sexual energy, but we are all called to transformation through discernment in how we express our sexuality within our given vocations (for example, married, single celibate, vowed religious).

Continence is the first stage in sexual asceticism. In this early stage, one refrains from sexual activity normally because of some circumstance, such as the death of a spouse, an extended illness, etc., rather than the absence of a desire. Religious celibacy or marriage is when the individual is governed by a vowed vocation. The celibate priest, monk, or nun renounces the fulfillment of sexual urges. God alone satisfies the person's deepest desires. A single celibate might make a private vow of celibacy and patterns this aspect of his or her contemplative life (a lifelong consecration) in a manner similar to a monastic. This path is different from continence as it is a calling from deep inside to go to God directly, without a partner. Married persons promise to have sexual intimacy with only their committed spouse.

Through the choice of a lifestyle, affirmed by taking "vows," the celibate or married individual avoids thoughts, environments, and circumstances that evoke sexual behaviors or desires inappropriate to these commitments. Celibates do not repress sexual desires; rather, they redirect these distinct and powerful energies in ways that evoke an even greater capacity to love God and others through selfless apostolic service.

Chastity, on the other hand, governs a person's innermost thoughts. All of us are called to be chaste, which is the interior discipline of refraining from, controlling, and avoiding stimuli (external and the train of thoughts) that are incompatible with our vocation. Few reach the ideal of chastity. The gift of equanimity on the thought of sex is rare. The chaste person usually strives his or her whole life to go beyond all physical expressions of sexuality, beyond all erotic thought, and even beyond subconscious desire. When one is truly chaste, a joyous state of freedom is reached even in one's nighttime dreams. The tradition promises the chaste person episodic or sustained experiences of peace and bliss.

The goal of a contemplative is to be naked, pure of heart, before God. The teaching from the elders endorses the contemplative one's efforts to come to God with an undivided heart. Union with God is deeper and more satisfying than sex. The word "vow" in Greek is the same word as "pay." In the literature it is a play on words: one pays their vows and vows to pray.

Chastity is individual heart work offered up in prayer. One of the fruits of a chaste life is to be innocent. Our souls are open and our hearts are not divided. We must never judge another but do our own inner work. We are always beginners, as sexual thoughts live beneath consciousness and can strike anyone at any time.

In the Hindu tradition there is a traditional way to move toward holiness through stages of renunciation deeply imbedded in the ancient culture of the people. The four stages of Indo-Aryan life are, first, the student; second, the householder; third, the retired person or hermit;

and, fourth, the monk or ascetic. In each stage, the goal is to move toward celibacy as a conscious effort. In other words, everyone is celibate at some point, whether married or monastic. The married person is celibate toward all others except his or her mate. Before and after the householder phase, there is a choice to move one's life toward transcending sexual consciousness for the sake of the spiritual life. The thought of sex no longer dominates one's imagination.

Much has been written about the appropriate practices to tame "sex thoughts." Our teachers commonly recognize that discerning our inappropriate sex thoughts at the first inkling, before they cluster into feelings or passions, is fundamental. If we notice them early, we can frequently redirect them swiftly. We dash them against the rock of Christ. Short arrow-like prayers to heaven, such as, "O Lord, make haste to help me," can be effective when one is directly in a battle with sexual thoughts and needs quickly to reverse the patterns of the mind. No matter what method is used, the practice is to notice the first indication of desire and, without commentary, to move it out of consciousness by laying the thought aside or saying a short prayer. Meditation is a skillful practice for the control of thoughts. It helps to work on our unconscious motivations and compulsions. Layer after layer of buried✓ inner debris of hubris flake off with steady practice.

The monastic tradition also advises using indirect means for subduing this passion rather than directly confronting it because the sex drive is so powerful and lies beneath consciousness. Cassian recommends fasting and ceaseless prayer. Engaging in physical exercise, keeping distance from the person who is the object of desire, and examining one's dreams are other examples of the indirect approach. In regard to dreams, spiritual direction has four guidelines: The first is to pray just before sleep. The second is periodically to practice all-night vigils. The teaching is to experience the night by keeping vigil over one's thoughts and to pray through the temptation in a periodic rhythm, thereby dispelling the challenges of night and darkness. The third directive is to fast and still one's spirit, rising early and rededicating oneself to prayer. Finally, one is to reduce any compulsive behavior, such as too much food or drink, that might catch one off guard.

Cassian wrote that it would be beneficial sometimes to require a monk undergoing the fires of sexual passion to take a day's journey from the monastery in order to reduce stress and allow the monk to return after such a journey to better relationships within the community (*Inst*. 6.3). This is a permission to be absent—not an expelling, a punishment, or an isolation technique. The monk sent on this journey is not to be denied Eucharist or coming to the table. The leaving is for the sake ✓ of returning. It provides time for the monk to work the passions down to a less compulsive intensity.

The practice of guarding the heart helps to offset the potency of sexual urges. When we guard our hearts, we prevent obstacles to prayer from entering our consciousness by placing our primary effort and attention at the entrance of our heart. This effort requires resisting encounters with people, places, and things that, after the experience, will linger "on one's heart." Such persistent ardors will interfere with our efforts to pray ceaselessly and eventually with our awareness of God's presence. We cannot engage in ceaseless prayer and simultaneously engage in afflictive thoughts and emotions. We must guard all of our choices to "be with" with God. The vowed individual makes an internal tryst with himself or herself and lays bare his or her secret attraction to another (as long as the person to whom one discloses is *not* the object of desire). The earlier this is acknowledged, the quicker the individual regains control.

Self-deception abounds. The practice of disclosing one's innermost thoughts to a wise elder is another helpful practice to avoid the tendency to deceive ourselves. The early monastics practiced manifestation of thoughts (*exagoreusis*), laying their thoughts out to an *abba* or *amma* (*Conf.* 2.10). This practice was the earliest form of spiritual direction. The elder would receive the thoughts and then give the monk a word, usually from Scripture, intended to break the cycle of obsessive thoughts. A wise elder is one who has tamed her thoughts and has compassionate understanding about how difficult it is to be pure in body, mind, and spirit. This elder needs to embody the spiritual teachings in order to mediate to others the meaning of life. If there is no wise elder available, the seeker matches inner thoughts to the teachings from the tradition as they are written in a rule or in Scripture. The role of the community is to embody the wisdom of the tradition so those teachings should be readily available.

What about self-sex? Is it an acceptable way to release sexual tensions? Cassian takes up this topic in *Institute* 6 and *Conference* 12, and the *Catechism of the Catholic Church* has a teaching on this in paragraph 2352. In summary, Cassian makes a distinction between masturbation and nighttime dreams that cause erections and emissions. I understand Cassian's teachings are not evaluating the gravity of self-sex as he is trying to *train* the mind toward purity of heart. An impediment to that objective is sexual images, even in dreams. The goal of a monk's training in chastity is to be freed even of nocturnal emissions.

When night arousals cease or are only from needs of nature, the monk has doubtless arrived at a condition where he is found the same day and night, the same in bed as in prayer, the same alone as surrounded by others. "He never sees himself in secret as he would blush to be seen by [others]"; nor does he act in such a way that the all-seeing eye should see anything in him that he would wish to hide from others. The monk says, "Even the night has become my delight." (See *Conf.* 12, esp. 12.8.5.)

There seems to be a clear directive in the *Catechism* of the Roman Catholic Church that masturbation is one of the major sexual disorders and that it therefore needs to be confessed in the sacrament of reconciliation if one wants to be in compliance with church law. This is not a moral obligation, however, as venial sins need not be confessed to be in good standing with the church. The *Catechism* goes on to say that the disorder might have pastoral reasons that diminish any moral guilt or impute the consequences of sin. Ordinary contrite personal prayer and penitential rituals at the beginning of Mass serve as "confession" for most sins and make us ready and qualified for sitting and partaking at the eucharistic table. The *Catechism* is both a juridical document and a pastoral text written for us to remain faithful to our beliefs and the teachings of our elders. It is a skillful means to inform our conscience, which for each one of us is our highest and inviolable inner law.

Rules and regulations that lead to blaming and labeling tend to engender a dysfunctional guilt rather than inform the mind toward purity of heart. Guilt has its own life cycle of violence. The judgment springing from this guilt grooves the negative attitude and behavior into our systems and energizes the very destructive emotion it condemns. The way out is to be ever so gentle with ourselves and to offer up our brokenness in prayer to the wondrous love of Christ. It is not by human effort but with God's mercy that we transcend our afflictive sexual thoughts and come to the abiding realm of chastity. The purpose of this writing is to retrieve the desert wisdom that puts the emphasis on Christ's grace and to give seekers effective tools that will assist in redirecting inappropriate sexual inclinations. These teachings put the burden on the person to be compassionate toward oneself as a member of the human family, to gently move self-centered motivation and sexual compulsions toward the benefit of the other. This is the wholesome adult shift from self to sacrifice.

So, how can we reckon with something being wrong and not have guilt? This is the formation of conscience that proclaims God's mercy more than compensates for our propensity toward evil. We, through grace, receive a heart that prays to have the strength, insight, and stamina to follow those inclinations prompted by the Holy Spirit. We acknowledge that God understands us, and this climate of compassion creates a gentleness and willingness to follow the impulse of grace. Jesus was also human and he knows our innermost thoughts and desires.

A rampant sex addiction that is closely related to masturbation is internet pornography. An objective of pornography is to masturbate. To cultivate an arousal without a responsible relationship is harmful. Pornography within a marriage diminishes love and trust from a sexually intimate relationship. Pornography outside of marriage is considered by some to be "virtual promiscuity." This can lead to sexual addiction when what began as an occasional use of pornography rapidly escalates into a habit. At the very least, this affliction reduces the participants in the pornographic images or films to objects for one's gratification. Often the "actors" in the films are underage, and the sex trade is regularly linked to prostitution and the growing illegal business of sex slavery and trafficking of women and children. To cultivate a virtual fantasy life toward the self as a habitual way of life cools one's life force and chills the body, mind and soul. Relationships risk failure to thrive.

The best approach for subduing sexual energy that rises, as in masturbation, is to prevent it by habitual healthy monastic practices. When these energies do arise, note the causes and circumstances and start anew with gentle compassion. The language of sin leads to guilt and anxiety that usually compounds the tendency. The language of celibacy, vocation, and striving toward one's desire for God moves the energies away from self and toward God. It is in being human that we are saved. The Christian door is through the incarnation where we are made good, very good.

The desert tradition teaches the monastic that to pray without ceasing one needs to dedicate oneself totally to prayer and live a lifestyle that supports the dominant work of the contemplative life: to pray always. One therefore cannot take on the obligations of an intimate relationship with another person. For the single contemplative, the interior life cannot be consumed with seeking a mate rather than seeking God.

Even gender consciousness must be transcended for the sake of a spiritual life with God. Gender is a distinction that can be helpful or harmful in social networks. We need to use our gender for integration and transcend to a consciousness of God's presence rather than a self-consciousness of our particular gender. The whole debate of sexist language in worship is helpful to prevent domination and subservience, yet the object of worship is God, who is neither male nor female. Silence and ritual action go beyond words and can be effective means of evoking the presence of God. The Word became flesh through the incarnation of Jesus from the womb of Mary. The gender of Jesus is male, but the doctrinal burden in the person of Jesus is that he became human. The Word, who is God, was spoken and became Jesus of Nazareth. This Jesus is the Christ. However difficult it is, we must continue to strive gently for inclusive language that has universal intent. My own prayer is to the Holy Spirit, who groans within as I am praying for help. The word "paraclete" has its roots in a young suckling calling out for safety, food, and relationship.

In Christ there is no male or female, no distinctions among us that divide our love for one another. We accept others as they present themselves. It is good to have a firm grasp on one's sexual orientation so that the mind can refrain from confusion and fantasy. All of us are called to chastity—to be pure in mind and body. Another way of saying this is that no one has the right to abuse another for self-satisfaction.

Chaste thinking is a practice, not just a fruit, of celibacy. The more one grows in sweet patience, the more one grows in purity of body. The further we remove the passion of anger from ourselves, the firmer will be our grasp on chastity. The heat of the body will not cool unless the outbursts of the heart are restrained (*Conf.* 12.6.1). Sexual energies have a purpose in the spiritual life. These energies, when transmuted, return to the body and heighten other energies that at once quicken the heart for ardor, zeal, and self-donation. They also stabilize the mind for study, clear thinking, right action, and meditation. So, it's back to discernment as to the kind of energy one wants to store in the body.

The disciple who has sublimated his or her sexual energy has all the benefits of sex and more. In all these matters, the mind attains a subtle purity and will experience an increase of devotion that is difficult to describe or narrate. Just as one who has not experienced this joy cannot conceive of it, so too one cannot express it when one does conceive it. If you want to describe the sweetness of honey to someone who has never tasted it, that person will still not be able to experience with his ears what his mouth has never tasted. Likewise, those who have experienced the joy of the taste can only wonder at it within themselves. Thus, one with a quiet mind is inflamed with the words of the psalmist: "Wonderful are your works; that I know very well" (Ps 139:14).

Cassian describes the heavenly infusion of spiritual joy by which the despondent spirit is quickened to inspired gladness: those fiery transports of the heart and the ineffable and unheard-of consolations of joy by which we are sometimes aroused from an inert and stupid torpor to most fervent prayer, as from a deep sleep (*Conf.* 12.12.6). It can take weeks or years, but once God grants the gift of freedom from the struggles of sexual thoughts, a period of calm sets in, and the fruit of chastity is abiding. A heart that is not divided is at peace.

Third Affliction of the Body: Thoughts of Things

Like food, things are just another thought. We are not our things! We divert our attention away from God when we give our heart to things and make them our idols. When too much time and energy are used in acquiring and managing things, it snuffs out the spiritual life. We have a right relationship with things when they facilitate a God-given purpose. The illusion of personal ownership needs to be rooted out. We shift our thoughts from acquiring more and better "stuff" to becoming co-creators who use things as vessels on God's altar. A monastic regards all utensils and goods of the monastery as sacred vessels on the altar. He or she is neither prone to greed nor wasteful, and the tools of the altar are not neglected. Everything is gently used with moderation, with humility, and in obedience (RB 31.10–12). A lay contemplative can adapt Benedict's Rule to his or her occupational situation and personal life.

The anatomy of a thing thought is similar to food thoughts when they take on a life of their own. Things beget one thing, more things, better things, securing our things—and having enough money and resources to protect and care for our things. The train of restless, grasping thought continues and feeds on itself. This pattern of thinking is an illusion because we possess no "thing," and, as such, things will never satisfy. Is there any way out of this cycle of thought and acquiring? Yes, we must replace the grasping with a true belief that all comes from God as gift in abundance and must be returned to God. Things are on loan, and we must use them wisely with the permission of the Creator. In other words, the antidote is shifting the thought from ownership to reverence for God. The Genesis myth of the Garden of Eden was about things that were plentiful, lush, and well ordered. The test was to be content with what was given. We are put to the same test in our little earth gardens. When we do not receive gifts in gratitude and return them to our Creator, our grasping actions cause us to be cast out of the garden. We join our personal sin to the primordial sin of our ancestors.

The monastery is a unique culture where the original divine order in the Garden of Eden myth is ritually played out. We are clothed by the abbot or abbess. As monastics, we seek permission to use things as tools in service of our assigned obedience. We receive things given in obedience and reverse our tendency to grasp and hoard them. We hold each thing lightly, gently, for as long as it is given for our use; then, freely, we offer it to another for his or her use in apostolic service and labor. We leave all—our former way of life, status, entitlements, rank, and possessions—for a second Garden of Eden. The abbot or prioress, in the name of the community, bestows things, and we have all our needs met through the rituals and practices of humility and obedience.

A sign of returning home to the garden is to put on new clothes when invested with the monastic habit, a new garment of baptism. Because avarice is a learned vice, we receive strong preventive teachings concerning things. These teachings are based on the earliest accounts of good Christian communities that are described in the Acts of the Apostles: all things are to be used for the whole community and especially for distribution to the poor. Monastics are to live in such a simple way that the community can offer goods to the poor in the community's name.

Lay contemplatives also use as their guide the Acts of the Apostles by questioning how many things, and of what quality, are needed for making their dwelling or business a healthy, holy place to live as well as to be of service to the larger community. The poor provide an opportunity for the layperson to use discernment about personal and communal things. For example, in light of my needs, when do I have enough? Those who have been blessed with prosperity must live in such a way that the poor are served in apostolic love, outreach, and the sharing of God's gifts. It is not an option for a Christian to ignore the poor.

Like all thoughts, the thing thought needs to be rooted out over and over again. To be in the world and not of it necessitates practices that counter the prevailing world condition of consumerism. To succeed in this endeavor the ordinary seeker should stay involved in a Christian community or another group that values sharing goods, reaching out to the poor, and caring for the goods of the earth. Above all, one should pray for discernment about the right use of things for the honor and glory of God. This redirection of one's thoughts and actions repays a greater joy than the satisfaction of a single thing. All is gift.

We can never be complacent when it comes to things. The thing thought can return after years of humble living. Through lack of vigilance or increased needs of old age or some other period of insecurity and anxiety, we begin to take back things. Our works are done for self-gain and not for the community or for God. We once again live on daydreams of having more things or more travel and other entitlements. In this relapse of faith a monastic may leave the monastery or a parent may leave the family to pursue and care for his or her own things. The thing is once again the idol and instead of not being able to live without God, the person can't live without things.

One answer to this breakdown is a return to a balanced work and prayer life, noticing the beauty and order of God's creation. This state of gratitude and continually walking in the presence of God returns the seeker to a state of equilibrium where the desire for things has no grip. In this state, the householder or monastic once again accepts that things can never be owned; they are tools for the work of God. This shift from doing work for things to doing the interior work to deepen our relationship with God in prayer (*opus Dei*) is ultimately the work of God (*ora et labora*) and returns us to Eden.

In our times, this grasping for things can come in the form of "things to do" and conceptual to-do lists that grab us from the inside. It could be the "too many," "too much" of relationships, hobbies, electronic social networks, virtual conversations, and compulsive curiosity. When one's consciousness is things or anything other than God (as in prayer and devotion to the inner purity of heart), this is an affliction of something other than God, an idol.

Both householder and monastic must refrain from attachment to things. Instead, we make personal resolutions and vows to follow a "rule of life" that makes it a habit to remember God. Afflictive thoughts about things obscure that memory. Reduce "things" and God springs up. We can use things as mirrors. In each thing we can see and remind ourselves of God. Then we will not act or use things as if they were God. As seekers, we desire to walk in the presence of God, not in the company of stuff. We accept all gifts in gratitude, tend to them graciously, and share them through our life's work, which renders them sacred for ritual and holy worship. This mindfulness not only roots out thoughts of things but also frees us from worry and anxiety.

First Affliction of the Mind: Thoughts of Anger

Thoughts of anger arise in each one of us. The good news is that anger is a learned response and, as such, can be unlearned and entirely rooted out. Anger passes quickly, even if it rises frequently and habitually because of life's ups and downs; however, we can learn to see it and resist its power. God is never the cause of our anger. The desert elders teach that anger disqualifies us from spiritual work because our capacity for love is diminished.

The adverse consequences of anger are many. Anger diminishes insight and wisdom. Anger dims and dulls the mind. Inner blindness no longer employs right thinking and acting. In this volatile state, the phrase "blind with rage" is more literal than symbolic. The angry person perceives information poorly and projects it back on others by starting quarrels and, in the process, loses the esteem of others. Unchecked anger can lead to depression and sometimes madness, even if only temporary. In community and society this contributes to universal disharmony, at times even leading to bodily injury and murder.

The most compelling indictment against anger is that it shrinks our spiritual relationships with self, others, and God. We no longer have the capacity to discern. The seeker's ability to discern spirits when evaluating choices and making decisions is the fruit of a clear mind, so we must not hold on to even a "little" anger. One cannot justify that the scope or seriousness of an injustice mitigates the teaching about letting go of angry thoughts. When angry, the soul is inaccessible, and there is no teaching about "righteous anger" in the desert tradition. In the face of injustice and oppression, the only option is a compassionate, nonviolent response.

The goal of a seeker is purity of heart. We were created by God and our desire is to return to God who is love. Angry thoughts that linger place an obstacle between us and God. Once in the grip of anger, we must, in order to see God again, still our thoughts (*apatheia*) and rest with a calm mind in the heart. Origen uses the term "active life" to refer to the work of letting go of one's thoughts while positively practicing virtue. This is the work of asceticism. He describes the "contemplative life" as one of pure prayer. The contemplative knows God by reason and also by emptying the mind of all thoughts of God (*apophatic*). Similarly, Evagrius defines prayer as both "lifting up the mind to God" and "the expulsion of thoughts." One's mind must be pure and clear to move from the stages where all thought and images are purged to the illuminative stage, where one's mind is filled with the light of the Holy Spirit, a state of spiritual ecstasy. With this teaching in mind the catechesis on anger is clear: anger does not befit the chosen vessel called to seek God.

Cassian spoke about six ways to offset, reduce, and ultimately rid the seeker of anger:

1. Vigilance: Keep vigilance over the heart and do not permit anger, even for a moment, to enter.
2. Reconciliation: When we have done wrong or even if we perceive that others have felt wronged, we should reconcile with them before the setting of the sun. We ask for forgiveness because we are one body, "for anyone's loss is a loss for all of us" (*Inst*. 8.14).
3. Memory: In addition to letting go of the anger, we should root out even the memory of the wrongdoing. The practice is to forget as many times as it takes to move the anger thought out of consciousness.
4. Relationship, not Solitude: The practice is to face the anger but stay in relationship rather than isolation. It is wrong thinking to entertain the idea that if only I didn't work or live with so-and-so, then I would not be irritated. The anger isn't out there; it

is an inner beast and needs to be banished. Even in solitude an afflicted person can be angry at a rock.

5. Freedom: Abbot Moses taught that it is impossible not to be accosted by thoughts, but it is in the power of every earnest seeker either to welcome them in or to reject them. He recommends frequent reading of Scripture and regular singing of psalms to keep the mind in virtue (*Conf.* 1.17).

6. Recollection: Preferring and cultivating thoughts toward God to worldly concerns of attraction or aversion is called recollection. A wonderful section in *Conference* 10 about thoughts says that whatever I think about before prayer comes into church with me. If I can't lift my heart and mind to God, then prayer is not possible. The directive is to get ready to listen to God.

Cassian reinforces these six themes with the teaching about controlling the mind and stilling thoughts. This is achieved by the practice of noticing a thought and then unthinking it by letting it go and replacing it with a sacred word or image. This quiet, wordless intention was articulated a thousand years later in *The Cloud of Unknowing*. Prayer happens in the silence beyond thoughts, words, or images. Moving toward purity of heart is simply having a clear mind without thoughts. In this pure mind, charity springs up without effort.

Seeking God in every corner of one's thoughts is discernment. The search leads one to sort thoughts and ask whether they are from God, self, the devil, or other harmful outside influences. Test and see which thoughts add beauty and grace and which ones are deadly: "Beloved, do not believe every spirit, but test the spirits to see whether they are from God" (1 John 4:1). Things are not always what they seem, as partial truths can be deceptive. It is therefore wise to get the whole picture and ensure you have the right motivation. Helpful to discernment is the practice of manifestation of afflictive thoughts (*exagoreusis*) to a wise elder as well as sorting the angry thoughts (*diakrisis*). If the seeker does not separate and make distinctions early in the process, confusion follows, and instead of having a discerning heart, he or she has a fuming heart. No spiritual practice should be motivated by rage.

According to Cassian, friendships thrive on virtue and harmony and are divided by anger. Real friends want, and refuse, the same things. Equal in goodness, they renounce thoughts of anger. Both *lectio* and friendships strengthen the desire to meet God face to face. The gift of friendship, says Abbot Joseph, can only last among those who are of equal goodness. They must share like-mindedness and common purpose. They never, or hardly ever, disagree, or if they do differ, it is in matters that concern their progress in the spiritual life. But if they begin to get hot with eager disputes, it is clear that they have not dealt with their afflictions. For if they have truly renounced their thoughts, then they could listen to another's thoughts without scorn (*Conf.* 16). Frequent quarrels cool love: friends first part their hearts, then their shared time and place. This is no surprise since anger fosters the road of adversarial thoughts, desires, and passions.

Thoughts will come and thoughts will go, but we have the freedom to consent or not to consent to our thoughts. Our consent is key and the good news is that with spiritual practices and God's grace thoughts can be redirected. Like a snake's head, we notice when anger rises and how the thought feeds upon itself. Before the snake strikes, we must catch the angry thought at the first inkling of awareness and replace the afflictive anger with thoughts of God.

The experience of days, months, and years without anger brightens the eyes, clears the skin, and quickens the walk of the seeker. The absence of anger enlightens the mind. I can more easily read the books of nature, Scripture, and experience and see clearly that my friends are manifestations of God. An ineffable joy replaces gloom, anxiety, and calculating about details of life that swing out of control. When we reverse anger, we imitate Christ accepting the role of self-sacrifice and we consent to lay down our life for another. To endure unjust persecution is the cost of discipleship.

Second Affliction of the Mind: Thoughts of Dejection

Dejection that often leads to depression is a condition provoked by thoughts, just as thoughts control our inclinations toward anger. Unlike anger that is to be calmed no matter its source or force or size, the cause of depression designates the appropriate treatment. While depression is often caused by anger that has gone deep into the unconscious level of our mind, there are other sources. It is good to sort out the causes of depression because the way in to this state of mind is a clue to the way out.

Unresolved anger caused by harm inflicted on the dejected person needs to be anointed with reconciliation and a return to daily forgiveness: "Don't let the sun go down on your anger." Harm can harm again and again through memories in thoughts and feelings like resentment, regret, and cynicism. These memories need to be shifted to prayer, asking for mercy for all involved.

Another cause of depression is grief due to the loss of a person, a thing, our bodily well-being, or some change that was not our choice. With grief, one must begin the long process of letting go of a loved one or a cherished dream. The remedy is to accept the mercy and compassion of God and community and in gratitude to choose life every day. Healing comes in time and by God's grace. The desire for gain that has not been realized or the loss of hope in the future is another form of grief, and these dejected thoughts need to be met by conversion to more realistic expectations. If I live in the past or future, I miss the grace of the present moment.

There is also depression that has no apparent reason. The depression that comes out of nowhere is often chemically based and needs chemical therapy under the care of a medical doctor. Other times dejected thoughts are clearly caused by us through the burden of personal sin.

Honest contrition, making amends, and confession of sin in the sacrament of reconciliation can work wonders for peace of mind.

Another type of dejected thinking that has no apparent reason is existential dread. It is characterized by a dark mood and a desire "not to be." This thinking is offset by accepting the human condition as it is and realizing that the personal source of such feelings may not be one's own; rather, what does matter is what one makes of this mental suffering. This dejected thought of undifferentiated dread just is. Thoughts can be noticed. Thoughts can be healed with the individual choosing, in freedom, life and wholeness over sadness. This dread can be both personal and collective (the being caught into the web of the culture that has dishonor as its way of being). To realize what is normal for all humans swimming in our human condition and my place in the universe requires courage and sturdy faith that all is redeemed by God's saving grace. The cross is real, but Christ Jesus who saved us is our source of abundant grace and lasting hope now and in the things to come. There is a grace to accept the situation and a patience to undergo the hardship.

Dejected thinking that leads to self-denigration is actually a perverse form of pride in need of God's mercy. We are dejected because we are not receiving from others and from ourselves the praise we deserve. Here, the person may think more highly of oneself than is the reality. In all humility (truth), derogatory thoughts need to be replaced with honest self-appraisal and realistic expectations. When the self is offended, then humility is the antidote.

Finally, dejection may also be an honest fear of death. Transformation in the heart of Christ with renewed faith that death has been conquered through the cross is the spiritual way out of this depression. Through the door of mortality is eternal life.

Five practices plus recommendations for training:

1. Stay in relationships. To isolate when depressed can lead to more confusion.
2. Amend faults and correct manners.
3. Refrain from thoughts that lead to self-destruction or suicide.
4. Refrain from and redirect any and all thoughts of putting oneself down.
5. Resist morbid suffering; "not to care" needs to be replaced with patience, which is self-donation.

The training on rooting out dejection is similar to the teachings on other afflictive thoughts. Cassian advises us to catch it early. Notice your thoughts, and when a sad thought begins say, "It just is: I feel sad. I count on God's grace." Then redirect the thought out of consciousness. In short, check it early, dispatch it, dash it on the rock which is Christ. Since this kind of depression and sorrow rises from the unconscious and can lead to deadly despair, utmost compassion needs to be the first concern. One must remember that there is always a way out. The alternative to self-abuse or suicide is forgiveness. Christ has overcome all evil, sadness, and even death itself. If I am not my thoughts, neither am I my moods or feelings.

One benefit of dejection is that for some folks sincere grief for wrongdoing softens the hardness of heart. This, in turn, may lead to compunction, which fires up our desire for God. Compunction is wholesome sorrow. Dejection is unwholesome sorrow and it replaces the fruits of the Spirit. They cannot coexist. So, how can one discern the difference between compunction and dejection? Dejection cycles round and round about harm done to me. Since dejection resides in the subconscious, the dejected person needs compassion, because it is difficult for him or her to achieve complete peace of mind even after conversion of heart.

Detachment from painful experiences is not indifference and it is the preferred way of thinking. When we are dejected, we must let go of and change parts, or the whole, of a lifestyle that is sinful. Even if chemically depressed, one can practice faith in the mercy of God. In the end, there are fruits from our periods of dejected thinking. By staying hopeful even in darkness, one is aware, moment by moment, of the true nature of reality. Dejection also weans one from the physical senses and awakens the spiritual senses. For example, a depressed person may enter into the contemplative mystery and have a taste of seeing without images. This undifferentiated reality is the experience of the dark abyss of nothingness, which empties all that is illusion. When

darkness lifts, we see the beauty in the smallest trifle—
even the dazzling darkness of emptiness.

The Hinge Affliction: Thoughts of Acedia

Acedia is really a hinge affliction: the third affliction
of the mind and the first affliction of the soul. *Acedia* is
recognized by a great weariness of the soul. The seeker's
ability to discern sleeps. He or she is separated from reason and awareness (*Inst.* 10.4). This toxic fatigue puts
the soul to sleep. *Acedia* is easy for others to detect in
another person, but it is hard for the afflicted one to
own his or her hardness of heart and the temptation to
get off the spiritual journey. The mind is sluggish, and
thoughts are slow and diminished. There is an irritabil-
ity of spirit, profound boredom, and discontent toward
one's current condition. *Acedia* shows itself in distaste for
spiritual things. Scripture and spiritual reading are re-
pulsive. The ability to notice thoughts is gone—replaced
by a bad mood. There is an overwhelming pull to ignore
one's spiritual practice and to "give up," to surrender
in hopelessness. The tragedy of *acedia* is that I could die
while I am not really living. While dejection leads to
suicide, *acedia* leads to soul-death ("soulside") when the
seeker rejects continuing work on the spiritual journey.

It is difficult to exaggerate the seriousness of *acedia*
for the practitioner who has abandoned a former way
of life and renounced afflictive thoughts of body, mind,
and spirit. The serious seeker who has completed all this
training and who practices fasting, vigils, discernment,

and prayer suddenly denies (through spiritual lethargy) his or her committed life with God. The psalmist describes the affliction of suddenly stopping one's relationship with God as the noonday devil: "the destruction that wastes at noonday" (Ps 91:6).

Cassian identifies *acedia* as a secondary thought because it is a thought "about" thoughts. The practitioner is in a crisis of spiritual fulfillment and doubts his or her motivation, intentions, and reasons for doing sacred work. What's the use? This noonday devil lies in ambush when there is no return—no satisfaction or consolation— from the spiritual practices to give the seeker strength. This period of life is dangerous as temptations multiply to just "give up" and return to a self-centered life. The seeker may leave a monastic community, profession, marriage, etc. In the grips of *acedia* a seeker may even try to start one's own monastery (church), become a bishop or abbot, or transfer to another community.

Cassian describes this period in the practitioner's life as having a soul that is sick, asleep, and weary about doing anything good or bad. The thought of *acedia* produces a dislike of the place and the members of the community. This disdain evolves into contempt, public disdain, and faultfinding. The person afflicted may seek to go away from the monastery frequently, and he or she shirks monastic or apostolic work. Other symptoms that Cassian describes are sleeping all day, discontinuing personal and common prayer, and the inability to stay in one's cell or to do *lectio* (*Inst.* 10.3).

The afflicted seeker believes that the monastery or other spiritual community is preventing spiritual progress and romanticizes a distant "perfect" monastery or community. Leaving would be a heroic virtue. If the afflicted person stays, unfortunately, the restless mind and soul cause restlessness in others. Or the individual merely exists, with no energy. If the person leaves in a state of *acedia*, he or she will start an exterior life once again but not bring the practices of the interior spiritual journey. The afflicted soul is asleep, with no capacity for contemplation or insight. A soul that stays in this state is making a choice away from salvation and certainly from sanctification.

Cassian advised his monks who were plagued with *acedia* to rededicate themselves to all work—manual labor and spiritual practices. Check the temptation to think you are more spiritually advanced than you really are. Your spiritual practice is just now at the place of its transforming power. Start over as if you are a novice with the training of fasting, guarding the heart, manifesting and sorting thoughts, discerning prayerfully, keeping vigils, and observing common life. Reverse the tendencies that spring from *acedia* by doing the opposite of what you feel. For example, if you feel like aimless roaming, stay in your cell, avoid idleness and laziness, resist traveling and restless visiting, work mindfully, eat and drink mindfully and moderately, be content with assigned work, stop activities that give permission to skip community obligations and personal practices, avoid others with the same affliction, resist chatter, and return to silence.

Other recommendations include the following: Work honestly for others who are in need as it checks desires for possessions. Resist those who give gifts because gifts reinforce an autonomous lifestyle rather than supporting one's economic commitment to the community and family. Likewise, refrain from public work until a measure of selflessness is obtained. Then, the service is truly for the "other." Refrain from taking too much time "for yourself" because, instead of receiving energy, idle time can easily kill your industriousness, perpetuating spiritual sloth—therefore, study and be quiet (*Inst*. 10.7.3–5).

The effects on the monastic community of severe cases of *acedia* can be significant. *Acedia* is an illness, and kindness should be shown. But just because someone is sick, we should not become ill ourselves. *Acedia* is an infectious disease for a group, and the leadership must take action on behalf of the group. A monastic afflicted with *acedia* might actually try to persuade others to leave while he or she stays. This manipulation should be resisted. In fact, Cassian advises the monastic not to keep company with one who is afflicted with *acedia*. The group sets boundaries as a starting place for dialogue. A wise elder is sent to extend compassion delivered with apostolic sternness. The group members should keep the boundaries. Two further teachings are stored in the sections on *acedia* and its remedies: the cell and compunction.

Practice of the cell. How does the practitioner afflicted with *acedia* "stay" and work through this time of spiritual dryness? The most important ascetic practice for *acedia* is solitude and sitting alone in the silence of the cell. This is done not for the sake of being alone but for the intention of being with God. This is the practice of the cell and the place of the cell is the teacher. This is where I memorize psalms and study Scripture, practice recollection and pray without ceasing, or refrain from working to rest and to meditate. Overwork is the biggest obstacle to seekers moving into the kind of prayer that is absorption into God, beyond images (see *Conf.* 9).

The cell is a personal place where simplicity reigns, where my mind and soul can breathe and listen in the daily and seasonal rhythm of the *horarium*. Here, I slow down my thoughts, one at a time, and truly know that I am not my thoughts. This personal sanctuary is more than a safe haven, for it keeps me faithful to my commitments even when zeal wanes. In this sacred place, I sleep, surrender, and experience the night. My cell also reminds me I will die, and this personal bodily death is something I must do alone. So there is no running from this cell, no denying death.

The gift of tears: Compunction. *Acedia* creates a dried up, hardened soul. Tears of compunction soften us and prepare us to begin again. Compunction, says the *Philokalia*, is the state of one who is "pricked to the heart," who has become conscious of his or her distance from God and yet has an altered awareness and ardor for God, the heart's desire. Once again, the heart softens and there is a feeling of sorrow, tenderness, and joy springing from sincere repentance. It's a burning state, like being in love, not a reaction to an incident. Compunction resolves *acedia* with a heightened relationship with God that has no moods or periods of doubt. One feels like a sinner in constant need of God's mercy. Fear of God is the beginning of wisdom and is a right relationship with God. This is well-ordered humility for a creature toward the Creator. Compunction purifies and causes us to come closer to God in love through remorse. One is naked before God without shame or guilt. Pierced to the heart, only one's relationship with God matters. If *acedia* is not negotiated, one can pass into the affliction of vainglory.

Second Affliction of the Soul: Thoughts of Vainglory

Vainglory is doing all the right things for the wrong reasons. Vainglory is taking credit for good actions. "Glory" means "God's presence," and the vainglorious person takes that presence to mean "self" rather than "God." Shifting all my attention toward self is an affliction of motivation. It is a secondary thought, as it is what I am thinking when I do something. My vainglorious thoughts are about what others think about me; in this way, I actually perceive myself through what I think others think of me.

Many spiritual directors as well as the afflicted one cannot detect vainglory. We deceive ourselves and conclude that we are holy and spiritually advanced. This affliction may prompt us to become leaders in spiritual and public professions. Vainglory is the opposite of dejection. In the one, I put myself down; in the other, I puff myself up. Both are forms of pride, not recognizing or accepting reality as it is. Humility is to be neither too high nor too low.

Vainglory is presumption when I act out of overconfidence. Vainglory replaces God with "me" as the object of worship. If glory is the experienced presence of God, then we cannot appropriate the glory for ourselves. Adoration and reverence are proper to experience God in one's interior life. If I take to myself what belongs to God, then there is no veneration, only illusion and vanity. Glory, when given to God, glows with the light of the Holy Spirit. It is palpable "presence" and "beauty." Shame is the inverse of glory, a terrible knowledge of our destiny, the awful nakedness we feel without the garment of light. Glory is the way the living God is known. Glory is the way it is when we see in faith. Sometimes in prayer we actually see our souls with our physical eyes. It has light, color, and subtle movement. When we see God, it is more. We use the word "glory" to describe it. We can't exaggerate how important it is to see through the eyes of faith that has all matter clothed in God's glory.

Vainglory attacks the spiritual side of serious seekers. It is a wound of the spiritually proficient who have mastered the earlier afflictions of food, sex, things, anger, dejection, and *acedia*. These afflictive thoughts, ever so quietly, twist the truth in order to move toward self instead of toward God. It is like saying, "I am so virtuous

I don't need God anymore. I can do anything." This attitude is dangerous to the soul. If a stilled heart is full of self, then the spiritual powers of keen insight and single-minded concentration can outwardly look good but be brutally devastating. If I foster vainglorious thoughts, I appropriate to myself what belongs to God.

Vainglory is an illness that attacks from both the right (good impulses) and the left (negative impulses). On the right I flatter myself about my "perfect" practice. Everything about me looks good from the outside: *my* dress, voice, vigils, fasts, prayers, reading, practices, obedience, silence, and display of outward humility. Vainglory attacks on the left by glorying in one's failures. Even if bad—no one is as bad as I am. To be the worst sinner is to glory in one's wicked ways. I, more than anyone else, am in need of God's mercy. Either excess good or bad when attributed to the self is vainglory and puffs up the ego. One who is afflicted with vainglory may indulge in daydreams about grandeur and public acclaim, or of having been rejected. Both are forms of vainglory, which intoxicates the mind. Any thought of envy is vainglory because one takes to oneself what glory properly belongs to another.

Vainglory is subtle. It has the ability to turn virtue into vice. For example, even my "middle way" in fasting is better than anyone else's moderation in fasting. Vainglory can deceive or even cause delusion. I'll not pray in front of others because they will think me holy. So then I don't pray at all. It's better not to do the practices because

I'll do them poorly, and they will become vices, and so I'll not do them (for example, fasting, vigils, and manifestation of thoughts). In this way, vainglory is an affliction that may wind itself through all the virtues, turning true humility into vanity. In this sense, vainglorious thoughts can subtly permeate all the gains of previous ascetical work and may disqualify the person from ministry.[8]

Recommended actions for one who has vainglory. As one progresses in the spiritual journey, discernment is absolutely essential, especially with vainglory, because good things look bad and bad things look good. Discussing this confusion with a seasoned elder is always a good starting place. Through sharing the practices, the elder should probe the motivations, discover the root causes of the thoughts, and help bring clarity to one's intentions. Be vigilant in overcoming vainglory because, after phasing out the affliction, one feels confident and superior, and this self-satisfaction is worse than the first affliction. Refrain from any thought that one has evolved past the spiritual practices and no longer needs fasting, prayers, guard of heart, watchfulness of thoughts, etc. If one is beyond them, then an outside authority must confirm it, because from the inside one would never know. A guide should confirm that the person is ready for a strict meditation practice and training of the mind to do prolonged silence and protracted solitude.

Rather than rushing into public work, refrain from any public role of ministry, because that would enhance the external viewing of oneself from the point of view of others. There is the danger that the positive feedback the afflicted one receives from others will be appropriated to self and not to God. Refrain from imagination, daydreams, and the excessive remembering of situations where one is the center of attention. Practice watchfulness of thoughts; stay in the present moment. Notice subtle signs such as boasting, being competitive, telling remarkable tales about yourself, seeking and taking credit, playing the role of the hero. In short, always edit, redirect, and change the thoughts about self that are either high (praise) or low (dejection). The practice of humility is to think about myself exactly as I am.

Watchfulness or vigilance over my thoughts is a specific practice that will anticipate situations or inklings that engender either grandiose thoughts or low self-esteem. Guard of the heart is a practice that turns even the potential of an afflictive thought into thoughts about prayer. In this way, prayer is a barrier to unwelcome thoughts. Another antidote is to return to a practice of ceaseless prayer. When prayer is automatically going on, vainglory cannot coexist. The words of the Jesus Prayer are particularly powerful to offset vainglory and pride: "Lord Jesus Christ, Son of the Living God, have mercy on me, a sinner."

In summary, to be seeking self-esteem rather than an all-out pursuit of God is contrary to the spiritual life. To move away (and stay away) from vainglorious thoughts of self and to shift the focus on God and others, we have to practice the simple but difficult work of dealing with our thoughts by guard of the heart, watchfulness over our thoughts, and vigilance in ceaseless prayer. "Watch and pray" is what Jesus said to his disciples at the end of his earthly ministry when they went to the Garden of Gethsemane. If I consent to vainglory and take credit for my good actions, all the forces of pride emerge. Pride is, without a doubt, the most dangerous of all the thoughts that become afflictions.

Third Affliction of the Soul: Thoughts of Pride

About carnal pride. There are two kinds of pride: carnal and spiritual. Carnal pride is human lack of discrimination when acting on inner conversations about the afflictive thoughts of body, mind, and spirit. Carnal pride gives me thoughts of exaggerated self-importance and is common to everyone. There is a self-willed defiance along with self-talk, for example, "Just this time," or, "I need this more than someone else," or, "I'm worth it." I begin to think that things that would be wrong for another to do are permissible for me, since I am good. My reference point is my own thoughts, desires, and passions, not God. I simply live for myself. Vainglory has to do with what others think and my own perception of that governs what I do, but pride has to do with my very being. Pride is who I think I am.

In pride, each thought gets distorted: I don't share food, I lust for others' affection or things, I seduce someone for my own pleasure, and I grasp things without consideration for how much is enough or what other people might need. I am also justified in my anger, believe I am above others, and put people down. I devote more time to self instead of to my spiritual practices. I may think, "Living is simply too much effort, let alone keeping my prayer life," which leads to a collapse of the training of my thoughts and a return to myself. God's word isn't defied as much as it is forgotten and dismissed as "not for me." Carnal pride is different from spiritual pride because the self takes precedence over God. Spiritual pride actually places the self *as god*.

About spiritual pride. Spiritual pride is a sin of the proficient. Once this person was turned toward God in thoughts, words, and deeds. Now the person turns only toward the self. This person's internal reference point is self-centered and not God-centered. This person acts as if God does not exist. Spiritual pride is a radical defiance with grave symptoms that involve audacious thoughts against God—even hatred and teaching against God and other believers. The spiritually proud have powers, including spiritual influence and abilities, that they use confidently in their "own name" and for their own benefit. If I am spiritually proud, I use my power to condemn and hurt others when they get in the way. Because I decide what is good, I appropriate the law to myself and use it in such a way that others fear my domination and punishment. God can be damned, for all I care. Hell doesn't exist, and if it does, I wouldn't want to be on the side of a God who creates hell.

The end stage for those afflicted with pride is defiance. The same person who renounced his or her former way of life, and all the thoughts of the former way of life, and who has all the powers of the practices and training of the mind now takes thoughts back toward the self and eventually toward evil. In this shift back, the prideful person decides that his or her thoughts can determine the Good, equating self with the Good for all. No discernment is necessary since the defiant one believes he or she is God.

Sadly, where once there was prayer without ceasing and mindfulness of the presence of God, now there is only self-adoration. The ego-self rises up and identifies with the culmination of the thoughts: gluttony, lust, rage, things, despair, boredom, vainglory, and pride. The defiant one then gets an invitation from the evil entities that promise to deliver double powers and strength. Subtle end-stage arrogance replaces any reverence for another's dignity. The narcissistic self is commander in chief and takes the place of God. Sometimes the prideful person bows to the Evil One, who now holds God's place, determining the moral good and demanding worship and adoration.

How can pride be detected? Cassian describes the indicators of pride in *Institute* 12.27. One symptom is a lukewarm spiritual fervor. The practitioner may not have fully renounced his or her former way of life or may have returned to old patterns after a full renunciation. My outside demeanor is rough, not gentle and kind. I consider myself above my peers. I determine what I need so I deny myself nothing. My eyes are dead. My heart is dull, and I have a flat affect. I am socially bored and become a taker rather than a giver. Restraint is not even an option because I now feel my earlier life was senseless.

The prideful practitioner is impertinent and scorns authority because he or she knows what is best. In fact, this person will be troublesome in taking directions or supervision except when he or she gets a self-serving order. A person trapped in carnal pride has an outward gait more like a strut and a loud, dominating voice with a noisy and excessive mirth that is ostentatious. If the person is silent, it is a bitter silence, an unreasonably gloomy mood. This person speaks with authority, answers with rancor, is too free with the tongue, lacks patience, and is "chatty." This person freely hands out insults but is fainthearted in receiving slights and unforgiving in receiving admonition. In short, a person afflicted with pride is stubborn about yielding to others, is never ready to give up self-will, and always seeks selfish ends. This person gives advice freely, but not according to the teachings, and has renounced traditional wisdom. This is the same person that once renounced their former way of life, renounced their afflictions, renounced all thoughts of God that were not of God, renounced thoughts of self that were not the true self. This person now renounces the way of life that is the spiritual journey of renunciation. This person renounces not only spiritual practice buy also renounces God. This is blasphemy.

Humility reverses pride. When we have the pride affliction, we go up the same twelve steps that we descend by way of humility (see RB 7). Most persons afflicted with pride don't want to be rid of it because it feels good to be right. Part of the end stage of pride is feeling sacrosanct—having no need of repentance, conversion, or change of heart. We know, however, that God's mercy as granted to the "good thief" can prevail, even at our last breath. It is prudent and humble to start all over on the spiritual life as a novice.

How can the affliction of pride be rooted out? Use the three guides: (1) teacher, (2) teachings (stored in Scripture and writings), and (3) traditions as lived by others (community) on the way.

A helpful starting place is to establish a good order in things and thoughts and then in relationships. Find a good teacher who has mastered the eight thoughts. Don't rely on gray hairs, but notice if the teacher has afflictions that are not resolved. Return to the practice of the eight thoughts. Renounce extremes and live a discerned life in the middle way. Do the practices of the cell, ceaseless prayer, compunction, discernment, fasting, good zeal, guard of the heart, *lectio divina*, manifestation of thoughts, manual labor, present awareness of God, recollection, silence, vigils, and watchfulness of thoughts.

Confess one's sins and receive absolution. Make amends. If we sort our thoughts and practice manual labor, the cell, ceaseless prayer, common life, and apostolic service, our prideful afflictions will be purified and replaced with humility.

Obviously, if one is in captivity of the Evil One and enmeshed in ontic evil, there is the need of the rite of exorcism that can be done by an ordained priest with these faculties. It's very serious to undergo an exorcism, and sometimes it takes several months, maybe years, to detoxify the soul. Thank God it is rare that there is genuine possession, obsession, or infestation of the Evil One in a sincere monastic. It is wholesome to fear evil and take precautions shunning any opportunity for the Evil One to contaminate persons, places, or things. We make the sign of the cross and say the Our Father with full intention and sincere humility.

One can see that in the light of the affliction of pride the practice of humility needs to start early, often, and always in the spiritual training. Katherine Howard, OSB,[9] translates St. Benedict's chapter 7 on humility into contemporary language. The Rule requires:

- reverent mindfulness of God
- watchfulness over behavior and inner thoughts
- desire to live in harmony with God's will
- willingness to respond to others' legitimate desires and commands out of love for God
- acceptance of suffering in life
- resistance to anger and depression or the desire to run away in the face of difficulties
- acknowledgment in our hearts that we are no better, and could very well be worse, than others

- living in community without the compulsion to project our unique identity by acting contrary to others

- refraining from speaking on every topic, in every situation

- avoidance of silly, sarcastic and demeaning laughter

- presenting oneself simply, gently, with a quiet and nonostentatious bodily demeanor

The first fruit of overcoming pride is a heart capable of meeting God "face-to-face." Earthly time is dedicated to loving God through the path of unknowing. If I am a serious seeker and I know my thoughts and renounce them, God as God emerges. The spiritual senses open and awareness awakens.

Benefits of Passing through Each Thought

When we pass through one of the afflictions, we can look back and see the benefits, the fruits that emerge on the other side, purging each of the afflictions.

When the thoughts get stilled and lose their binding power as afflictions, there is *apatheia* or purity of heart. Life is full of manifestations of God because the spiritual senses are awakened. The heart is warm, and there is a personal experience of God from the inside. Discernment is living from the mind that is descended into the heart. That still, small voice rises with grace, courage, and poise.

About food and drink: To eat the middle way is not only healthy for the body's weight, energy, and longevity but also the first step in living a life of discrimination—being able to sort, to anticipate my "enough," to feel the equanimity of being satisfied, of absences of urges dominating my consciousness. When I eat and drink mindfully, with poise and appreciation, I experience the fruits of transcending the compulsive affliction of the food and drink thought. Fasting becomes a way of life and feasting is the way I celebrate it!

About sex: To be continent, celibate, and chaste is to be in right relationship with my vocation. To hold the sacredness of the other and to be treasured by my community or my marriage partner or to enjoy being single is to be fully human. I am the same in the day as I am in the night. Sexual energies quicken life and all its living.

About things: To be a gardener on this planet earth is to breathe and to work. I use things because of what I do—art, crafts, nature, reading, cooking, enjoying the entire universe. What I have for my use is enough. All is good, very good. "Things" become who I am. I am rich indeed! I take up my responsibility to preserve things for the next generation's well-being and prosperity.

About anger: After my emotions are quieted, I have the facility to see the other's point of view and experience compassion. The forgiver and the forgiven merge. I become an elder with bright eyes, clear skin, a quick step, and a gentle smile. Others are attracted to me, but I am at peace in my cell. Forgiveness reigns. No past diminishes my present and no future supplants it.

About dejection: Mystery rises in place of dense fog and weighty sorrow. A smile relaxes my brow. In place of darkness, I see luminous, clear, and intense light. My spiritual senses open. My experience of depression is lifted, and my thoughts become quiet. On the other side of mystery, I know that I know and am known.

About *acedia*: The hard heart melts into compunction, and the gift of tears cleanses me and takes me beyond returning to my former way of life. The cell becomes the home of my heart. My work is my prayer and my prayer is my work. Ceaseless repentance becomes an abiding experience of mercy. All is well. I am stilled. There are several benefits from the afflictive thoughts and suffering of *acedia* if one adheres to the above practices and purifies the intention in faith rather than in self-interest and consolation:

- Once again the beauty and health of the practice of manual labor is seen.
- The seeker is trained to recognize that work and prayer are interchangeable.
- The sacredness of the moment is experienced.
- In ceaseless prayer the mind is increasingly stilled, chatter stops, and layers of consciousness surface.
- In the silence of not speaking (taciturnity), we learn to listen, rest, receive, observe, and live in the present moment.

- Restfulness of mind is restored with the rhythm of the work of the body.

- Mood swings shift to a moderate and acceptable range.

- Once the mood becomes more settled, a new feeling emerges: compunction.

About vainglory: Glory is God's. My self-centeredness actually dies. Only God satisfies. Public ministry or manual labor is equally my preference since God is at work in me and I am not the one doing it. Either success or failure is all right. I have a single-minded energy; inner fantasies no longer influence me. All is God's way and that is my way. There is no separation.

I can discern motivation for apostolic service. Embarrassment is overcome since the response to failure or accomplishment is neither high nor low: interior poise emerges. One can work in either ministry or the monastery because the inner work is the same.

Watching thoughts is a discipline whether alone or with others. The cloister and the cell can be interchangeable with work and social obligations. There is no need for a desert if one has overcome vainglory. A solitary life is helpful to know my thoughts; the practice of watchfulness can be a mental substitute for the desert culture of a monk or a hermit.

Confidence in myself is placed securely in confidence in God; there is no practice of "self-assigned" virtues. I lay aside thoughts and give God glory (ceaseless prayer), and God raises up the virtue necessary for my situation.

The practice of compunction is to give God glory and ask for mercy for oneself. Interior dialogue is away from self-chatter and toward God. Christ consciousness emerges. The I-thought continues to "watch and pray."

About pride: Pride is doing the wrong things for the wrong reasons, but humility replaces gluttony, lust, greed, anger, depression, *acedia*, vainglory, and self-righteousness. Purity of heart is our default place of rest. All harsh and unhealthy fears are at peace. We renounce our former way of life; then we go deeper inside and renounce our afflictive thoughts that put us at risk to return to our former way of life.

When the ego relaxes its grip from holding us toward the self, we enjoy the True Self of being made in the image and likeness of God. Christ-consciousness replaces our ego-consciousness. Beyond ego-consciousness, we enjoy a mind at peace. Purity of heart abides, but humility is what others see.

Ceaseless prayer maintains the warm, devoted heart that has compassion toward others. The self empties out through Christ. But this gets ahead of our story. The battle with our thoughts happens over and over again with more subtle invitations. Now that we have seen how seductive the thoughts are, it is wise to catch them early, often, and with humble expectation. I am not my thoughts! The work of sorting thoughts is called discernment.

Chapter 2

Tools for the Interior Journey

Antidotes: Rooting out Afflictions

No matter what the content of the thought, there are six helpful antidotes. The first one—and the most helpful—is to watch our thoughts. This observation, this looking at our thoughts from the outside, is the most powerful antidote. We keep vigil; if we watch over our thoughts and guard our hearts from easy entry in the first place, then there is less to root out.

Second, we notice the earliest rising of the thought. This is why the teaching on the anatomy of a thought matters. We need to catch it early. We notice the triggers and replace that emerging thought with another thought. Our brains cannot maintain focal consciousness on more than one thought at a time. We can think quickly, and it might seem like multitasking or that it's simultaneous, but the brain really has the power to focus on only one thought at a time. The best thought is a prayer, like, "O God, come to my assistance; O Lord, make haste to help me" (see Ps 71). Another arrow prayer can also be used, such as, "Help," or, "Jesus, mercy." But it should be routine and the same prayer each and every time, as we do not have the poise to think it through at the moment of temptation. So the thought rises and we lay our prayer over it. We do this over and over again, gently and routinely, so that the chain of thoughts simply takes leave like a vapor.

A third antidote is to have a ceaseless prayer practice like the Jesus Prayer and raise it to consciousness when the thought comes to light. This ceaseless prayer practice has the benefit of doing inner work on the unconscious zone of the psyche so that thoughts are detained or sorted out before they come to an invitational stage.

The fourth antidote is to combat the invitation. This inner method of the self talking to temptations was originally a teaching about using a quote from Scripture or another inspired book to offset the inclination to evil. In our times, this is risky because *antirrhetikos*[1] ("talking back") might give us the opportunity to fall into self talking to self, and this direction often lacks the discernment of a wise elder.

A fifth antidote is to return to the present moment and rededicate oneself to the vocation of duty or the selfless service required by one's circumstances. This total attention has the power to break the train of thought and return one to original resolve without the drag of ambiguity.

A sixth antidote is to come in the back door of the affliction, anticipate its strength and seduction, and offset its power with a vigorous practice that prevents the trigger from providing a starter. Examples of these practices would be to totally clean one's cell, workshop, or studio; to make a pilgrimage to a holy place that takes one out of one's environment or a potentially risky situation. One could take on a radical obedience that would require time, effort, and care for someone else. One could exchange the habits of time, place, and circumstance that trigger the affliction with an alternative: anger with compassion, dejection with care for tender plants, food with table waiting and washing dishes, disordered sexual urges with wholesome other-centered friendship, *acedia* with extra duty of manual labor, vainglory with invisible service and lowly tasks in service of the group, pride with providing care for others before one's own needs are met. Sacrifice, rightly ordered and with egoless agenda, does ascetical work to calm the soul and extend this gentleness and compassion to others.

I have learned the hard way that there's no substitute for taking seriously one's own afflictions, as they are given to us to help us begin our spiritual journey. Over and over, too many times to count, I dismissed reports of nagging afflictions that brought this person or that person to Beech Grove for a retreat. Sometimes it took years of dialogue to convince me that the stories of grief were the moments of revelation of God. Now, I listen more attentively. These afflictions are "teachers" that rise up from our very own experiences. There seems to be no way to skip them and make any lasting progress.

The benefit of raw attention to our afflictions is that we are compassionate with others because we know how difficult it is to make changes in our habits and to sustain preferred ways of acting. We have help though. The Holy Spirit groans within us and brings to mind what we can do to be free of these compulsions. There are tools of prayer that can root out and keep out the deepest afflictive patterns. There are three degrees of training to make these tools prayer: observance, practice, and *praxis*.

To listen with the ear of the heart takes a lifetime of discernment. The monastic way of life is designed to provide training and a protective environment to seek God. This is done through exterior and interior forms. The novitiate is meant to be an immersion into training and practice of discernment that continues through the monastic's lifetime. Discernment leads to right action and aligns our daily life with the Gospel message. All monastic practices require discernment to maintain the middle way. Discernment, the sorting of our thoughts, is the basic foundation of all the practices. This work is our side of the relationship with God. Then, prayer springs up! We continue with teachings about this inner work, asceticism.

Tools of Prayer:
Observance, Practice, and *Praxis*

We Benedictines observe the Rule of St. Benedict. When you come into a monastery, you observe the life in common with shared things, table, and worship. The schedule (*horarium*) is an expectation to be taken seriously and personally, as in individual observance. Permission is necessary if one needs to be absent. Practice is even more important than observance. Each of the observances requires a particular discipline. Practices done within the environment of observance are the work of the monastery. *Praxis* is what you do with your mind while you do the practices within the milieu (observances) of the monastery. Monastic life is a particular subculture—in the world but not of the world. The reign of God is the real world that starts now in this broken place so laced with the human condition groaning under the strain of illusion and sin.

Praxis is what one does with one's mind that governs thoughts and emotions. *Praxis* would be stilling the mind and body. Both the mind and the body require discipline of thoughts. Thoughts matter! It's micromanagement, not macro-aspirations. The consciousness of where to direct the mind's eye stills the stream of mental images and the ever-shifting movements of the body.

There are three concentric circles or degrees of work for the sake of this contemplative life:

1) Observance is what people see and is something that is done.
2) Practice is the discipline done within the observance.
3) *Praxis* is the inner training of the mind that we do in the practice and within the observance.

For example, you come to the monastery, the cloister, or the retreat house (observances) and enter into the practice of silence. The setting provides the solitude that protects and gives boundaries to the practice of silence. Within the practice is discipline of the thoughts of the mind (*praxis*).

That we "observe" silence is seen exteriorly. For the "practice" of silence we set aside designated times, places, and degrees of restrictions. And within the solitude and practice of silence is the "*praxis*" of stillness. This *praxis* is total contemplative rest of the body, emotions, and mind. This is the inner work of the mind within the exterior observances and practices.

When a person comes to a retreat at Beech Grove, we request compliance with the norm of silence in the solitude of the monastery. Then, we give training on how to still the mind and emotions as well as how to still the body.

Another example of observance, practice, and *praxis* is *statio*. We stand outside the church and line up, maintaining silence with feet firmly on the ground (observance that one can see from the outside). Before processing into church for Vespers, we listen to the tolling bells (practice of place, time, ritualized gestures of profound bows to the altar and to each other). With our minds, we practice recollection, reigning in all our senses and bringing our thoughts to stillness of body and mind (*praxis*). With each toll of the bell, we ride out the thoughts to come to that place of the present moment, ready to enter the temple of worship.

The practices of any method seem to take on the following three stages:

1. The training stage: Here one makes strenuous efforts to make the method a habit. It is conscious even to the point of counting the times a prayer is said, setting aside special times, and having a rosary or other device (such as journaling) to help the habit become deeply embedded in one's consciousness.

2. The practice next reaches the virtual stage: Now it's on the mental level, deeply embedded in the mind. This mental stage works for sustained periods seemingly without effort, but then it subsides and there are cooling periods. Soon the practice feels as if it is a pattern for life, but no. One must then go back to the habitual practices. This is the genius of practice. It is both the prayer, since on it rides the intention of union with God, and also the method to establish the human connections, linking body, mind, and soul with one's deepest desires.

3. Finally, there's the actual phase, when the method becomes a gift that abides through thick and thin. I suppose it's probably only at this level that one could say that one has Christ consciousness. This level is present whenever one thinks and knows that one is thinking.

✓ It does seem that there is always forgetfulness as long as we are human. Or it seems like there is mindlessness.

But the practice should endure no matter what. It brings
us back to our original intention and to that place of
consciousness that is shared, eventually merged. This is
why one must take up a practice and do it—continuously
and unceasingly until death. After a while, the practice
becomes automatic and moves along like a murmuring
brook or a flickering light through day and night. The
point is to sustain the practice until it has a life of its
own. In our case, God is our heart's desire and the life
we seek is an abiding awareness of the indwelling of the
Holy Spirit.

When the feeling of prayer reaches the point where it
becomes continuous, then spiritual prayer may be said to
begin. This is the gift of the Holy Spirit praying in and for
us, the last degree of prayer, which our minds can grasp.

Perhaps I should qualify the word "feeling." When we
are learning the interior journey and we have feelings,
emotions, and surges of ready energy, we soon learn that
these feelings are more subtle and less forceful than the
usual feelings we have for one another and for the work
we do in an ordinary day. These feelings are sensible
but soon come from a different source than our normal
psyche. These feelings are real, ready, and available but
are not the same as our surges of attachment and aversion. The spiritual energies are a different kind rather
than degree. When you have a practice that becomes a
prayer, these subtle energies rise and abide.

Yet, to pray mechanically and with a cold stare at some
religious object is not enough. We can learn to warm

the heart and stand in ready expectation. Prayer is a relationship, not a conceptual "thinking about God." Discernment teaches us how to pray in, with, and through the Holy Spirit, who is Uncreated Energy that quickens, warms, and enlightens us. This warming the heart is part of the work of the monastery, which is to pray always.

Seven Practices That Become Prayer

Discernment is a learned skill more than a system of theories. Habits of prayer have to be encoded and refreshed daily in the routine. Since the goal of the monastery is to seek God, the practices of prayer are essential. The common prayer of daily Eucharist and Liturgy of the Hours (Divine Office) makes our time holy. Yet, if the individual monastic does not cultivate a personal prayer habit, the common prayer can become perfunctory and an empty form. The Catholic identity has many cultural signs and symbols, but membership is not enough; there must be the inner connection with the body, mind, and soul of the individual.

Discernment requires a practice of ceaseless prayer so that listening with the ear of the heart has an ongoing method to operate and integrate the heart in one's daily life. In the Christian tradition there are many prayers but only a few practices that shift consciousness into this deeper restructuring of the mind to pray always. One is invited to one or many of these prayer practices that form the habit of continuous prayer from the inner heart. Here are seven of these practices that were embodied in saints, and we have writings of their teachings. Benedict's master teacher, John Cassian, devotes three conferences (9, 10, and 11) to the theory and practice of prayer. This fourth-century literature recommends the hard work to remove the afflictions, still the mind, and let prayer happen to the monastic. Benedict would presume every novice would know these teachings. I have found that, while I need to know these foundational prescriptions, it is helpful to invite the student to engage in an actual practice of prayer. There are many practices of prayer in the Christian tradition. It is important to do one of them for months and months so that the experience of self-acting prayer becomes a habit. Learning about prayer is no substitute for praying. As a child I knew prayer but then was taught prayers. It has only been in recent years that I know prayer again because of the invitation to bend low and go through the humble door of practice. This kind of knowing is not learned from reading books or going to church, even five times a day.

The Practice of the Presence:
As Taught by Brother Lawrence

Brother Lawrence was born Nicholas Herman in 1611 in the Province of Lorraine, France. After military service, he became a footman in service of the treasurer of France. Wanting to give his life to God, he first became a hermit. This he found too depressing. For ten years, he suffered guilt, unwholesome fear, and dread of God. He renounced methods of prayer that contributed to his depression. In his later thirties he joined the Carmelites in Paris. He was assigned kitchen duty. He found formal prayer tedious but discovered the practice of the Presence while he did manual labor. He offered his whole memory, imagination, and interior world to God. This became his mission. He taught it to all who came to the kitchen or his shoe shop. We have fourteen letters he wrote and his funeral eulogy and maxims that were collected by those who were taught by him. He died at the age of eighty-four.

Brother Lawrence has inspired us to practice, to renounce all that is not God. It's a practice that is easy to teach but not easy to sustain. Practice of the Presence is a scandal because it seems too simple: Brother Lawrence had no harsh judgment toward anyone who did wicked deeds and was surprised that people were so good because he was profoundly aware of his own tendencies to do evil. He said that he didn't need a spiritual director but a confessor.

This practice is comprehensive. When I first taught it, I thought it was more of a short prayer, an arrow prayer practice similar to John Cassian's "O God, come to my assistance." But now I see that it quickly leads to a total shift of consciousness and ceaseless prayer. Practice of the Presence initiates colloquy and renounces all that leads us away from God. When we stray, we return over and over again. Then, when we talk to God continuously, there is only God. This is faithing (a verb): To stop, direct my mind toward God. Say a prayer spontaneously, whatever comes to my mind. Then, I return to work. Then, I stop again. I stop often and remember God. Sometimes I say nothing, just nod (simple regard). I practice over and over while at work, walking, sitting, and standing; I even stop and practice at Mass or Divine Office. When I forget about God, I return promptly without any recrimination. We remember God's mercy.

The method of practice of the Presence is simple but profound:

- Think God in an image that rises (no set form)
- Think God when doing little things
- Do this or that for God, in God, with God
- Use all circumstances; nothing is too small for worship
- Adore, thank, greet, ask, and remain attentive
- Practice at all times and places, before sleep, upon awakening

Restart the practice when in mindless default thinking. This checks free-fall thinking and redirects thoughts to God. The method is simple: we act in faith that God never fails offering grace. We can count on God to remove our doubts. We change not our works but our ways of doing our works with faith. This purifies our motivation that governs our work. We look to God, offering our work to God and not to humans for praise or gain. The task and goal is to make our work a prayer. Prayer is sense-at-work in the presence of God.

Prayer and work become interchangeable, as the practice is continuous. When we are not working, our prayer is in the Presence so it doesn't matter which we are doing, prayer or work. There is no difference between the two.

Brother Lawrence speaks from experience. He recommends that we continue familiar conversation as often as possible, sharing all the details of our work as now being part of our prayer. He speaks of rising after a fall. Repent quickly and with no self-talk or commentary.

Never use prayer as an excuse not to work since there's no difference. Do one's assigned work for God's sake rather than change works and do them for our own sake.

The major teaching to practice the Presence is more than mindfulness and awareness or even concentration on the present moment. The object of the practice is to have faith in God, our Creator. This is a practice to make the sense of the presence of God habitual, not just from time to time. It seems that in proportion to our intensity of desire is the gift of the abiding Presence. We drive away all that is not thoughts about God. We keep our personal presence in the presence of our Living God. The Presence as a "wow" does fade into the ordinary. I'm not sure if it changes or if we metabolize the Presence and that it just feels so normal. But what does seem to shift is that there is no muddling of thoughts about God. There is a direct experience of God.

Brother Lawrence reports that "this presence doesn't take faith anymore." What I understand by this is that there is no doubt that holds place on my side when God's voice seems mute. What happens is that the voice is softer, softer and subtler as a presence. It's like being in a room where the wall at first seems white, and then I see it is eggshell or a slight lemon or has a hint of green. It is okay the way it is, no matter how it is.

Seek God by faith and not by favors, says Brother Lawrence. We are often quite satisfied with faith rather than stunning experiences of light and cosmic wholeness. Abiding faith is deeply satisfying. The experience that Brother Lawrence speaks of is that he's not sure it is even faith at all, as this is still that subtle abiding presence of God.

Those are the core teachings for this practice of the Presence. As I taught this to many groups over thirty years, questions rose, and from further study of the text these teachings emerged: we must discern that we need a practice to deal with our thoughts. Then, it seems to me that this particular practice is a great starting place to learn that we have thoughts and that it is this inner work that becomes prayer. Brother Lawrence repeats the dictum that God wants our thoughts, that God cares about our every thought and even receives our little "simple regard," our nodding to God from time to time, moment by moment. Our Lord accepts whatever prayer we offer and actually cares about what we think, how we think, how we feel, and how we act. It's reading about faith and too much speculation that misses the actual experience of God. How God is need not concern us, but that God is and is close to us is an abiding insight to remember. We lift up our heart and mind to God often, everywhere, and bow from the inside. Our God is personal and has offered us a relationship much like God relates as Trinity.

This is our real work as creatures. It doesn't matter where we work and where we live. It doesn't matter what we do but that we do every action with faith, in and with God. We renounce free-fall fantasy and conversations in the imagination. Can it be this simple? Is this not reductionism that mistakes the part for the whole? No, since we come with the whole biblical understanding of Jesus Christ embodied in the gospels. For our part, we engage our present moments away from self and selfishness toward freely offered sacrifice toward God through others.

The method is to lift up prayers gently, playfully, and spontaneously and to enter the Presence. God does the rest. If this sounds too good to be true, it does require much faith and a sustained effort. We begin to repeat this act of faith at the depth of the soul. Over time we merge into heart-to-heart communication with God. We are gifted with God's presence and communion happens. At this point, outside events rarely disturb the real peace that we experience. A gentle, loving gaze becomes the way of living and God lights the fire.

Brother Lawrence teaches that the soul needs only to consent. Our soul speaks to its deepest Soul, the Holy

Spirit. This practice of the Presence moves from practice to a way of living the life given to us. We experience nourishment of our soul. This means that instead of the soul having a practice in the midst of its ordinary life, a shift happens: ordinary life becomes the practice. God expands our consciousness, and we see God everywhere, in everyone, and in everything, including ourselves.

While Brother Lawrence spent his days as cook or cobbler, he considered his main work "to remain in the presence of God with all the humility of an unprofitable, but nonetheless faithful servant." To all that would come into the back door of this friary he'd expound on the method. He'd encourage them to start now no matter what troubles they were having in prayer or in living a good life.

But he also said that it's not surprising how at risk all of us are on this human side; the good news is that we can still remain faithful without worry. He said to replace worry with practice: stop for a short moment; stop whatever you are doing as frequently as you can; moment by moment adore God deep within your heart and delight in God in secret. Nothing can stop you from practicing your faith. Talk to God. Notice God. Gaze. Shift your attention from your thoughts to your faith in God. The multitude of thoughts crowd in on us and spoil everything. Evil begins in our thoughts, so we must be careful to lay them aside as soon as we become aware that they are not essential to our present duties or to our salvation. Doing this allows us to begin our conversation with God once again.

This practice is not only for kitchen duty. We are to remember God at prayer. The practice is helpful because just being at prayer isn't prayer. Brother Lawrence fine-tuned the French preference for the practice of simple regard. This momentary glance is noticing God looking at me! He said to use our own words for our side of the conversation, and for God we just let whatever comes to our mind be the response: "Lord, bless my work!" or "Lord, bless my prayer." This kind of practice doesn't need a cell, a shrine, or a sanctuary. We make our hearts a prayer room into which we can retire from time to time to converse with God gently, humbly, and lovingly.

One way to call your mind easily back to God during your fixed prayer times and to hold it more steady is not to let it take much flight during the day. You must keep it strictly in the presence of God. As we become used to doing this over and over in our minds, it is easier to remain at peace during our prayer times, or at least to recall our mind from its wanderings. We talk about whatever is on our minds. Ask for grace, offering sufferings. Brother Lawrence invites us during conversation with others to lift our hearts toward God from time to time; the slightest little remembrance will always be very pleasant to God.

The practice is not so much about the conversation as it is an act of living faith. We talk to God as if God is here. Most of the time we act as if God is not here. This is a reversal and a change of heart that has immense consequences for our interior life. There are many benefits to this practice. We ask for help and then overcome temptations. We lead a life that is closer to our desire for God. If God grants it, sometimes we actually have a felt presence of God. This can last for days, weeks, or years. This presence kindles love. Our desire becomes sharply focused. We try to live and live only in the presence of God. And to some rare souls the practice of the Presence accompanies them through the sufferings of this life and even the stages of dying.

The practice of simple regard sometimes is a thought not of God but of pain. This very pain can be a prayer. Brother Lawrence provides teachings on how suffering that is used like a prayer can become redemptive. In Letters 11 and 14, Brother Lawrence shares how he embraced suffering, for as long and severe as it was given to make up for his sins and to purify his soul. He assured suffering people that God's work on their behalf is being accomplished though their time of trial. He was direct in telling them not to waste all their time on seeking a remedy but in surrendering to God's way for them. He also assured them of his prayers.

The Practice of Self-Abandonment to the Present Moment: Attributed to Jean-Pierre de Caussade

The practice of self-abandonment is usually attributed to Jean-Pierre de Caussade, but there is evidence that it is likely the work of Madame de Guyon.[2] Jean-Pierre de Caussade was born in 1675 in southern France near Toulouse. The work known as *Abandonment to Divine Providence* was believed to be a collection of de Caussade's spiritual letters and conferences circulated privately by the Visitation nuns.

There are many titles for the same work translated from the French: *The Sacrament of the Present Moment*, *Abandonment to the Present Moment*, *Abandonment to the Divine Presence*, etc., but it is the familiar 17th-century work attributed to Jean-Pierre de Caussade. Rather than get caught up in finding the authentic writer of this text I prefer that we know it and do it. It has been very powerful for so many Christians, Hindus, and non-creedal practitioners. It is particularly recommended for Catholics.

Since God is present in the moment and I can see only the present, I need to forget the past and fore-get (if there is such a word) the future. Past thinking leads to discouragement and anxiety, and future thinking leads to fear. Surrendering one's will to do the duty or necessity of the present moment is abandonment to God. This is another way to sort our thoughts.

If I am looking for God's will, I need to look at my life now. My state in life (vocation) now is God's will. I can trust this because in each previous moment I did the necessity of the moment. The teaching goes on to say that there is nothing small or trivial in the eyes of God. The moment itself holds the will of God for me.

This would be a risky statement unless we can presume we are leading a moral life. Confession is a natural beginning to have all conscious sin forgiven and absolved. From that moment on, we practice abandoning self and make intentional our desire toward God. We can trust this practice because God is embodied in the present moment.

If God is in the present moment, then we can trust that God is manifest in our duty. We participate in God through fidelity to necessity. This is a profound teaching. Duty is passive and active: passive is to do only what is from the impulse of the Holy Spirit; active is to do it whenever new directives come to our attention. So we do not do anything but what the impulse of the Holy Spirit dictates, and we do only what we understand as our duty in this instant.

The practice shifts our experience of God. At first we are in God, and then God is in us. We actually sense God in us acting through us and extending God's presence with our actions that are ordinary duty. This is such a profound distinction, so let me try to explain it: If we act "in God," apostolic acts are required, a rule of life is prescribed, and direction is provided. It is hard work and we do our duty. When the shift takes place, we experience "God in us." We become like empty clay pots with no utility of our own design. We are broken pieces thrown in the corner.

From time to time we are reconstituted and called out for some assignment. We follow because God leads. Being present with full attention is the practice: we do God's will moment by moment, and we surrender whole-heartedly any concern about fruits of action (outcomes). We place ourselves in God's hands and have no inner commentary about how we did and how what we did unfolded. We know not if we will be of any benefit to others or ourselves. All interiority and exteriority is God.

[handwritten margin note: 4/8/14 Hard to do!]

In both levels of abandonment, we disengage the intellect and affect from self-reflexiveness so that we attend to the necessity of duty. This practice of prayer is not a conversation or a mantra. This practice is no-thought, a selfless acting in faith. All will be well if we abandon ourselves to God. The abandonment in the present moment is the prayer.

Our part is to be present to the moment. This mindfulness can be done because the present moment is offered to everyone. This wonderful practice, abandonment to the present moment, avoids the problems of quietism since we take responsibility for right effort and performing our duty according to the prompting of the Holy Spirit moment by moment.

This practice of abandonment also avoids the distinctions offered through different prayer practices. It does not matter whether we prefer devotion in meditation or imageless prayer of contemplation. The actual present moment is the guiding method.

In the text the author writes with style and grace and repeats these recommendations many times. If we are to take up this practice, we refrain from thoughts of past or future because the practice is faith in the moment. In faith, we see God's signs in the present moment. In this very moment we see the hand of God and we submit to God's will rather than our will. We reduce our curiosity to see less and believe more. It is a practice of faith. We measure our results by abandonment and surrender rather than by outcomes. We humbly let God be the judge. I see only the now. God holds the big picture.

For ourselves, we expect mystery and limitations. It would be against the spirit and practice of this method to grumble, complain, or show signs of nonverbal resistance. This discipline of acceptance is not only exterior but also interior. We refrain from inner murmuring and outer grumbling. The present moment delights us. We see the present moment as opportunity for grace and mystery. It is our source of holiness.

The practice gains intensity and we begin to anticipate surrender and receive opportunities of surrender wholeheartedly. We practice docility and accept changes willingly. We ask no questions about God's design for us. The test of this practice is to accept humiliations as part of the path. We disregard our natural resistance and apparent opposition to the demands of the present moment. We are confident and count on God's grace. We know this grace follows along with our willingness to undergo difficulties. Our job is to attend to the now wherein we do our duty, as it is God's will.

In this path, we prefer to be hidden and ordinary, as anonymity helps us replace self with faith. There's a freedom here and low stress as we learn to do only what is inspired by the impulse of grace—no more and no less. All ambitions are ruled off the agenda. God's will, not our willfulness, is our abiding desire.

There's also no need to discern one's state in life: duty names vocation. Doing our duty now in the moment is more salvific than moving toward higher states in life like becoming a religious or hermit. We actually bring together our will, our intellect, and our imagination to a single point in the present moment. This one-pointedness of our decisions purifies our hearts. We do not become deadened with this practice because we are alert to change since each moment contains the Holy Spirit's guidance. Docility and supple readiness is our abiding disposition. In summary, we do our part and leave the rest to God. This one thing or thought at a time (done reverently) in this moment is God. We abandon self-made thoughts and receive God consciousness in the sacredness and sacrifice of the present moment. This is a high practice of faith. Since God is, we remain in silent adoration moment by moment. Then the moment ignites into presence of the Present One.

The Practice of the Cloud of Unknowing: As Taught by the Unknown Author of The Cloud of Unknowing

As befits the title of this work,[3] the identity of the author remains anonymous despite much speculation. Most theories suggest that he was a Cistercian hermit or a Carthusian priest. Regardless of status, the author's writing reveals a keen theological mind and a perceptive director of souls. The teaching reflects the *apophatic* or negative spiritual tradition, which emphasizes that God is beyond our thoughts, concepts, and images.

The author is believed to have lived in the East Midlands, a region of central England, during the latter half of the fourteenth century. The author contributed to an exceptional wave of spiritual literature, which emerged from England at that time, including the works of Richard Rolle, Walter Hilton, and Julian of Norwich.

In addition to spiritual teaching, the unknown author is highly regarded for literary gifts. The author's work displays remarkable strength and vigor in the original Middle English. Six other anonymous works are attributed to this author; probably the most well-known of these is *A Letter of Private Direction* (often titled *The Book of Privy Counseling*). I found *The Cloud of Unknowing* to be quiet accessible even though the content is abstract and dense. I tasted the distinctiveness of a mystical treatise that was originally written in English. Most of the mystical writings I studied before *The Cloud* were translations in English of Spanish, French, or German mystics. I feel that *The Cloud* is an inspired literature, not unlike Scripture.

We are all called to contemplation, resting in God. There are many paths in this journey. This path very specifically taught by the unknown author of *The Cloud of Unknowing* is for those attracted to the mystery and not inclined to go through images of Jesus or Mary or through the life of Jesus Christ as devotion. The attraction is Christ centered, but beyond the images and stories. The unknown author speaks for those of us who are invited to the *apophatic* (imageless) path and says, "God is a jealous lover; we must fix our love on God. Close the doors and windows on imagination because God is beyond our thoughts, concepts, and images."[4]

This practice is most helpful to train the mind to refrain from overidentification with and reliance on the thinking mind. We cannot know God, but we can love our Heart's Desire. The Holy Spirit can teach us how.

The teaching of the method is helpful and easy to understand but hard to do: the practice is to lift up our hearts to the Lord with a gentle stirring of love, to desire God for God's own sake, not for God's gifts. We must center all our attention and desire on God. Let God be the sole concern of mind and heart. We need to forget all else, feel nothing else but a kind of darkness about our minds. This is the Cloud of Unknowing.

We can't will ourselves to feel naked before God, but we can practice a "naked intent" toward God. If we just stay present here with the teaching, the meaning will emerge. This is delicate and subtle but intelligible.

The teaching recommends that we, in spirit, "cry out to God whom you love." We place our hope in feeling and seeing God as God is. This is a negative path: we unthink what we think about God so that God emerges in our thoughts as God is and not as we wish or fabricate God to be.

When we cry out to God whom we love, we do it often and always in this cloud, this darkness. We forget all else. This isn't just a pious recommendation; this is a directive to forget all thoughts racing in our minds. These thoughts are trampled down in the cloud of forgetting. In exchange, we receive God who brings us to deeper levels than ordinary surface consciousness. We come to a deep experience of God as God.

Writing in the fourteenth century, this unknown author gives us a method of practice. The author tells seekers to choose a single word, one syllable, but it should be meaningful to them. The word might be "God" or "love." We fix it in our minds so that it will remain there, come what may. We use this word to "beat" upon the cloud of darkness above us (the beat is more like the baton of an orchestra leader—steady beat, soft, measured—not like a baseball bat). This is how we enter the cloud. Now, all of us have thoughts rising from ordinary time, from below. What do we do with them? The author recommends that to subdue all distractions, we move them (consign them) to the cloud of forgetting beneath us.

We answer with this word alone to any thought that enters consciousness; we think not about the thought as the value lies in its simplicity (oneness). Contemplation is a way of knowing wherein one turns to God with a burning heart, with desire for God alone, and rests in blind awareness of naked being.

We are called to a way of being. This is how I understand this from my study of the desert tradition: We feel inclined to move into a deeper relationship with God as God—that is, renounce even our thought of God, because just as we are not our thoughts neither is God our thoughts of God. So we take our love for God in secret, as this is interior, and we take whatever level of purity of heart we might have and walk between this cloud of unknowing (we can't know God by thoughts) and the cloud of forgetting (we bring all our distractions to that little word of love that carries our intent of love) and repeat over and over the word instead of thinking any particular thoughts.

We love God for God's own sake. Another way of saying it using the image of a cloud (which means non-thought): Enter the cloud of unknowing by practicing in the cloud of forgetting all else but a naked intent of love using the sacred word.

Like most practices, this will make more sense when it is part of your experience. Descriptions fail to capture the simplicity and profundity of this way of unknowing. We would also attend to Scripture. We'd do *lectio*, but sit easily, using the words of Scripture like a mirror. The words reflect God, God's ways, and draw us into mystery. In this path, we are particularly attracted to the mystical voice of Scripture in the gospel of St. John or in St. John's epistles. We pray intuitively, not analytically; we let what comes arise and stand before it. This is not the study of a scholar. We let prayer rise; short prayer pierces the heavens!

During prayer we forget the self. By letting go (or letting thoughts be without accompanying them with another thought), we empty our minds and hearts of everything except God during the time of this "work." We refrain from other kinds of knowledge and processing other experiences. We want no less than God. We read down all thoughts of creatures beneath the cloud of forgetting.

In this kind of prayer, brute force has no place. We become more like a child. Our heart waits for the gracious initiative of the Lord. And God comes in prayer, like our naked intent, as naked too. There's usually no experience of consolation or desolation. We find consolation in doing God's will. If I can name one word that describes the experience of doing this kind of prayer, it is "subtle." There are just hints. We must be alert to receive them but without any expectation. We are letting God be God and letting our faith be faith.

Sometimes when we talk about prayer, we use words like "lift up our hearts" or "put our thoughts down" in the cloud of forgetting or "move into contemplation" or "out in gratefulness." All these words must be erased since interpretations limit God. The human side often describes God and conscribes God as too small, narrow, absent, or out there. We refrain from thinking this way in the practice of the cloud. Even the cloud can't be taken as a literal image.

We unthink but warm our hearts and send the word as darts of love. The stress on warming the heart is a later tradition and serves as a corrective to unrelating to others and being impersonal since the prayer practice is so impersonal. *Apophatic* doesn't mean being bereft of spiritual and full-bodied warmth toward God and others. All words limp before this awesome way of prayer.

All prayers, but particularly the practice of the cloud, stress desire, not results. We never get there; it's just a way of being before God. To be there (before God) we discipline the imagination so that we are not mentally someplace else! Our ordinary senses are not up to this level of receptivity, so we distrust our senses whenever we fix our minds on an image that represents God.

As we walk from here to there, our thoughts can safely pray this prayer: "That which I am I offer to you, O Lord, without looking to any quality of your Being, but only to the fact that you are as you are; this, and nothing more. That which I am, I offer to you, Our Lord, for You are it entirely. . . . That I am . . . that you are."[5] I know of nuns who do this emptiness practice using the refrain, "That I am, that You are." The author of the *Cloud* says, "So now forget your misery and sinfulness and, and, on that simple elemental level, think only that you are as you are."

You must stand at the door of contemplation and practice devotion of heart. Using your word, send your naked intent to our Lord in the cloud of unknowing. We said that there are many paths and not everyone is called to walk the same path. The practice taught in the text of *The Cloud of Unknowing* is a way to learn discernment. The training is rigorous and simple. Its focus on the "that God is" and the "that I am" empties the ego-self and the thinking mind so that the Holy Spirit rises and abides.

The Practice of Recollection: As Taught by St. Teresa of Avila

St. Teresa of Avila taught her nuns that God is within so they should bring all thoughts toward God. Recollecting is bringing in all the thoughts to our center. This form of sorting is living from the heart. The training in discernment is to focus attention on God dwelling within.

Teresa of Jesus was born Teresa de Cepeda y Humada in 1515 to a wealthy family in Avila, Spain. Beautiful, charming, and outgoing, she entered the local Carmelite convent in 1536. For some twenty years she struggled with serious illness and the somewhat lax religious life of her convent. Her spiritual fervor faded, and for a year she even abandoned prayer altogether. In 1554 she experienced a "reconversion" after seeing a statue of the wounded Christ.

With renewed ardor, Teresa eventually regained her spiritual equilibrium and emerged to conduct the reform of her Carmelite order. In 1562, she founded St. Joseph's Convent in Avila, the first convent of the Carmelite reform. A tireless worker, she founded sixteen more convents before her death in 1582 at the age of sixty-seven. Teresa's extraordinary insight into the process of spiritual growth has been transmitted through her writings.

The Life is an autobiographical work that tells of her own spiritual development up to the point when she founded her first convent. Works that present her spiritual teachings are *The Way of Perfection*, written for the sisters of St. Joseph's Convent, and *The Interior Castle*, her most thorough and orderly description of the spiritual life.

The practice. Recollection is a practice recommended by St. Teresa of Avila. She speaks of active and passive recollection. The right effort for active recollection is to gather in our senses and lift up our mind to God, she says.[6]

"Think of God when praying. I tell you that for wandering minds it is very important not only to believe these truths but to strive to understand them by experience." And she goes on to say, "What I'm trying to point out is that we should see and be present to the One with whom we speak without turning our backs on God, for I don't think speaking with God while thinking of a thousand other vanities would amount to anything else but turning our backs on God."[7]

She understood that harm comes from not truly understanding that God is near; instead, we imagine God as far away. Since indeed how far away are you? if we go to the heavens to seek God! Now, is your face such, Lord, that we would not look at it when you are so close to us? If people aren't looking at us when we speak, it doesn't seem to us that they are listening to what we say. And do we close our eyes to avoid seeing that you, Lord, are looking at us?

So, the first step of the practice of recollection is to think God as near rather than far away. This is our faith.

This alone is what I want to explain: that in order to acquire the habit of easily recollecting our minds and understanding what we are saying, and with whom we are speaking, it is necessary that the exterior senses be recollected and that we give them (our senses) something with which to be occupied. For, indeed, we have heaven within ourselves since the Lord of heaven is there.

So, we slow down our thoughts, think of God, and focus our attention toward God rather than review our thoughts or bring any concepts forward. God is within. All one needs to do is go into solitude, look within oneself, and not turn away from so good a Guest; rather, with great humility, one speaks to God as to a father or mother. Tell God about your trials; ask God for a remedy against them, realizing that you are not worthy to be God's daughter.

The Lord is within us and there we must be with the Lord. I understand the practice here is to turn our mind's eye toward our Lord. It's not exactly an image, but more tuning into a Presence.

We leave aside any faintheartedness that some persons have who refuse our Lord's invitations. St. Teresa tells us to take God at his word since Jesus is our Spouse and will treat us accordingly. Recollection is the moment wherein the soul collects its faculties together and enters within itself to be with its God.[8]

And the soul's divine Master comes more quickly than through any other method it might use to teach it and give it the prayer of quiet. Even though passive recollection might happen later in our practice, we will always need to return to active recollection from time to time. There's no one who is not a beginner.

Recollection keeps the eyes closed almost as often as the soul prays. We must strive not to look at things here below. This striving comes at the beginning; afterward, there's no need to strive. A greater effort is needed to open the eyes while praying. It seems the soul is aware of being strengthened and fortified at the expense of the body, that it leaves the body alone and weakened, and that it receives in this recollection a supply of provisions to strengthen it against the body and the mind's tendency to be scattered. Recollection is a withdrawing of the senses from exterior things and a renunciation of them in such a way that our thoughts are not attracted to exterior inclinations.

The eyes close to avoid seeing distractions and so that the sight might be more awake to the things of the soul. There's no need to think holy thoughts. God doesn't need them and often they take us into vainglory. Recollection in and of itself is the prayer.

There are, however, greater and lesser degrees of recollection. In the beginning, the body causes difficulties because it claims its rights without realizing that it is cutting off its own head by not surrendering. If we make the effort, practice this recollection for some days, and get used to it, the gain will be clearly seen; we will understand, when beginning to pray, that the bees are approaching and entering the beehive to make honey.

And this recollection will be effected without our effort because the Lord has desired that, during the time the faculties are drawn inward, the soul and its will may merit to have this dominion. Eventually when the soul does no more than give a sign that it wishes to be recollected, the senses obey and become recollected.

Even though they go out again afterward, their having already surrendered is a great thing, for they go out as captives and subjects that do not cause the harm they did previously. And when the will calls them back again, they come more quickly, until after many of these entries the Lord wills that they rest entirely in perfect contemplation.

When we get used to the practice of recollection and because there is no impediment from outside, the soul enjoys being alone with God. Since the soul is close to the fire, a little spark will ignite and set everything ablaze.

We must disengage ourselves from everything so as to approach God interiorly and withdraw within ourselves even in the midst of occupations. St. Teresa says that it is very beneficial to remember God all through the day, even if it is only for a brief moment. Eventually we realize that it isn't "necessary to shout" to speak to God; God will give one the experience of God's presence.

Recollection is not something supernatural but something we can desire and achieve ourselves with the help of God, for without this help we can do nothing, not even have good thoughts. To expect it just to happen is not realistic. We have our work to do on behalf of our relationship with God.

Recollection is not a silence of the faculties; it is an enclosure of the faculties within the soul. This recollection practice is a manner of praying that the soul gets so quickly used to that it doesn't go astray; nor do the faculties become restless, as time will tell. St. Teresa goes on to say, "I only ask that you try this method, even though it may mean some struggle; everything involves struggle before the habit is acquired. But I assure you that before long it will be a great consolation for you to know that you can find this Holy Father, whom you are beseeching, within you without tiring yourself in seeking where He is."[9]

Recollection lies within our power. It involves a gradual increase of self-control and an end to vain wandering from the right path; it means conquering, which is making use of one's senses for the sake of the inner life. If you speak, strive to remember that the One with whom you are speaking is present within.

If you listen, remember that you are going to hear the One who is very close to you when the Lord speaks. In sum, bear in mind that you can, if you want, avoid ever withdrawing from such good company, and be sorry that for a long time you left God alone, of whom you are so much in need.

St. Teresa goes on to recommend that, if you can, you should practice this recollection often during the day; if you can't, do so a few times. As you become accustomed to it, you will experience the benefit. Once the Lord gives this recollection, you will not exchange it for any treasure.

> Since nothing is learned without a little effort, consider, Sister, for the love of God, as well employed the attention you give to this method of prayer. I know if you try this method that within a year, or perhaps half a year, you will acquire it, by the favor of God. See how little time it takes for a gain as great as is that of laying a good foundation.[10]

These teachings and more directives from Teresa are from *The Way of Perfection*. In her systematic work, *The*

Interior Castle, she moves from active recollection to passive recollection, depending on which mansion the soul is dwelling in. In *The Interior Castle*, St. Teresa sets forth a gradual immersion into God and God into us. Here's a short summary of the teachings in *The Interior Castle* pertaining to recollection.

The dwellings. The castle is entered into by prayer. Prayer is the doorway that opens up into the mystery of God.[11] In the first dwellings, effort starts slowly as desire for God begins to supplant all previous desires.

The first dwelling: The soul says prayers but is still distracted and involved in worldly things such as possessions, honor, or business affairs. The soul prays on occasion.

The second dwelling: The soul begins to practice prayer and notice the prompting and invitation of Christ's grace that comes from external sources like books, sermons, friendships, and trials. The goal of one's strivings is conformity with God's will.

The third dwelling: The soul recognizes its desire to have its own experience of God. The soul begins ascetical practices to remove obstacles and start to practice periods of recollection. These persons use their time well and reach out toward their neighbors and fit their external life of dress and possessions with interior desires. They fear consequences to their health and have difficulty parting with wealth. They are shocked by the faults of others and are quickly distraught by a little dryness. They need someone who is free of the world's illusions with whom they might speak. Between the third and fourth dwellings is a shift in the practice of recollection.

The fourth dwelling: This is the beginning of the supernatural. Infused prayer happens. It is important not to think much but to love much. The right effort is to please God in everything, in striving, insofar as possible, not to offend God, and in asking God for advancement of the honor and glory of the Son. This contemplative prayer begins with a passive experience of recollection, a gentle drawing of the faculties inward; it is different from recollection achieved at the cost of human effort. This prayer of infused recollection is a less intense form of initial contemplation or, as called by Teresa, the prayer of quiet. While the will finds rest in the prayer of quiet, in the peace of God's presence, the intellect (in Teresa's terminology) continues to move about.

One should let the intellect go and surrender oneself into the arms of love, for distractions, the wandering mind, are a part of the human condition and can no more be avoided than can eating and sleeping.

The fifth dwelling: The soul has prayer of union wherein the faculties become completely silent. It has a certitude that it was in God and God was in it. For suspended times the soul is dead to itself and completely free. The marriage symbolism is used: the soul and our Lord become engaged, getting to know one another. The soul's effort is to attend to humility and service to others.

The sixth dwelling: This place moves the marriage symbolism toward betrothal. Courage is needed to endure both exterior and interior trials (opposition from others; praise; severe illnesses, inner sufferings, fears, and misunderstanding on the part of the confessor and consequent anxiety that God will allow one to be deceived; and a feeling of unbearable inner oppression and even of being rejected by God).

The sixth dwelling is characterized by spiritual awakenings and deep impulses. Woundings of love cause both pain and delight. Though the soul in ecstasy is without consciousness in its outward life, it was never before so awake to the things of God, nor did it ever before have so deep an enlightenment and knowledge of God. Illuminations teach the soul.

The distinction between discursive meditation about Christ and contemplative presence to him is the inability of contemplative souls to engage in discursive thought about the mysteries of the passion and life of Christ in their prayer; this is very common. But contemplating these mysteries, dwelling on them with a simple gaze, will not impede the most sublime prayer.

St. Teresa insists on staying in contact with Christ's humanity and divinity. The contemplative enters into the unity of her body, mind, and soul and does not transcend the body. Failure to do this stops progress into the last two dwelling places.

The seventh dwelling: There are no closed doors between the sixth and seventh dwellings. The unity of the soul is felt as natural (connatural). This place is in the extreme interior, in some place very deep within itself.

The grace of spiritual marriage, of perfect union, is bestowed. The goal of the spiritual journey is union with Christ, now no longer living as the divine *Logos* but as the Word incarnate, risen and connoted by the attributes of his earthly adventure, especially the resurrection.

The fruit of this marriage shows itself in good works. The interior calm fortifies these persons so that they may endure much less calm in the exterior events of their lives, that they might have the strength to serve. The works of service may be outstanding ones, but they need not be. One must concentrate on serving those who are in one's company. The Lord doesn't look so much at the greatness of our works as at the love with which they are done. God will join our sacrifice with that which was offered for us. Thus, even though our works are small, they will have the value our love for God would have merited had they been great.

The practice of recollection accompanies the practitioner, but a good sign is to reduce words, mental work, and involvement of the imagination. A spiritual director can assist with discernment. At first, it is important to have someone who has experience of recollection and discretion in judgment. Later, when there's experience of the mansions, it would be good to have a learned person who can detect truth and deliver us from spiritual practices that keep us at a superficial level. Reading is a great advantage in assisting us with recollection, centering our thoughts, and also raising up truth to match our experience.

Recollection is more important today with all the fragmentation of the mind because of our digital culture.

New skills are needed to tame the thoughts to prevent addictions and compulsivity in social networking, acquiring things, and overworking that causes fatigue and depression. Can we rein in our curiosity and all things new and discern the presence of the Holy Spirit within?

The Practice of Colloquy: Dialogue with Our Lord; As Taught by Our Lord to Gabrielle Bossis

This teaching comes from Gabrielle Bossis, a Frenchwoman from the twentieth century. There are other teachings of colloquy, but this is the best example of *how* to practice this prayer.

There are many saints in the Christian tradition who had a transcendent experience of God breaking in to their ordinary consciousness. Some reported raptures, wounds of love, visions, and locutions. None of those epic events describe the colloquy practice as I understand it. Colloquy as a practice is simply talking to God rather than talking to yourself. You sort your thoughts in the presence of our Lord and tell our Lord everything. Like being married, there are no secrets; all thoughts are shared.

For the purpose of sharing one such saint who used colloquy at the invitation of our Lord, we can learn from a little book first published in France called *He and I*.[12]

Gabrielle Bossis was born in Nantes in 1874, the youngest of four children. She had a degree in nursing, but her life work was writing, producing, and acting in entertaining comedies and morally pointed dramas. She was invited to many countries, including Canada and most of Europe. She resisted pressure to join a convent. She found her vocation using her talents of fine arts in the world. She also resisted marriage but did not resist being a wealthy woman with fine things and good taste. On rare occasions, she was surprised by Christ's voice, but it was from the age of sixty-two until she died on June 9, 1950, at age seventy-six that she had an ongoing dialogue with our Lord. He directed her to write a journal. She had an extroverted life of acting and being a celebrity, while she also wrote at our Lord's direction the fragments of conversations that were compiled into *He and I*.

It is a mark of authenticity that the entries are all about Christ's words to Gabrielle. We learn very little about Gabrielle. She's an instrument. What attracts me to this book over and over again is how our Lord invites and actually coaches Gabrielle to speak, think, and be with our Lord. It's a teaching into Christ consciousness. There are other books about Christ consciousness, but there is no better instruction that is available in English to each of us, should we respond to the invitation.

The first moment is an event that happens to us. We simply awaken to the real presence of Jesus. Then, we participate by sharing our thoughts with our Lord. We listen: locutions are made as if you hear him or as if through the imagination comes a "voice." We don't consider ourselves in a "for real" ongoing conversation. But we do "for real" practice of faith.

The practice is to shift the I-thoughts to sharing in faith with Jesus. Self-talk responses at first might be autosuggestion, but as we see in *He and I*, it later becomes communion. Another way of saying this is that our prayer is sharing all our waking thoughts. Desires are directed to Jesus. For example, we might be attracted to use the image of the Sacred Heart or the Good Shepherd or Jesus walking from Emmaus.

Whatever the image we are inclined to use, it becomes adoration. We remain in the Presence, sometimes sharing thoughts and other times in total silence. We stay still with a loving gaze. This is no one-hour-a-day event. Our daily life is accompanied with this inner dialogue with Jesus. All is shared. (Notice we don't bring Jesus to our daily life, as in intercessory prayer, but our daily life is the prayer.) All our work is done both really and symbolically for Jesus, in Jesus' presence.

The practice takes each impulse of grace and follows it consciously and conscientiously toward Jesus in love. While Gabrielle didn't care about stages of relationship, we can witness how she evolved, first as an acquaintance, then using the language of dear friends with our Lord, then deliberating commitment, and finally merging into union.

We note that Gabrielle accepted suffering as a test of strength to be firm in resolve. She grew in love of our Lord, and there was a natural shift away from protecting herself and avoiding suffering. She loved in such a way that the cost to her was simply a way of showing her felt love toward our Lord. She had a keen realization of how much Jesus suffered for us, and she felt the same inclinations to give of herself like Jesus gave of himself for us. Sacrifice becomes part of the exchange.

This practice trains the will. Her consent is to notice the subtle requests in each impulse of grace. Her "willingness" was to do the will of the Beloved. She strove to focus her attention to imitate Jesus, to follow his directives, to focus on his love, and to be loving in return. Intimacy abounds.

Imitation gives way to cocreating with our Lord: doing work on behalf of others. This ranges from little acts of kindness to picking up other's suffering on behalf of their salvation or sanctification. Intercessory prayer is dynamic and productive.

We see that her outward "work" or apostolic service is only to do God's will, not to get anything done. For Gabrielle Bossis, work as an artist was real, insofar as she did much good, but it was also a medium to give form for her relationship with our Lord.

She was vigilant to regard herself always in need of God's grace. Her own effort did not establish this close relationship. She had a profound sense of otherness and separation from God and potentially of being a sinner. She practiced guard of the heart continuously so as to be worthy of this inner dialogue with the Savior. When she failed in some way, she simply and humbly named the act and asked for forgiveness. No waste of time on her own feelings of guilt as she desired only our Lord's intimacy.

This intimacy was mediated through signs, like birds and sunsets. These were received as "flowers" of the beloved. Rich exchange was normal and everyday, like lovers are wont to do. There was a charming exchange between our Lord and Gabrielle when Jesus says that she should address him not as "The Lord" but as "*My* Lord."

We see signs that her *lectio* was on our Lord's life as depicted in the gospels. There was no great mission for France during her life, like Joan of Arc. With Gabrielle, it seems that the *colloquy* itself was the message rather than her writings, one-act plays, handiwork, or any projects. In fact, Gabrielle is not a saint. I've never met anyone who knew her. There is no cult around her. Jesus taught her a method, the practice of colloquy.

The title *He and I* is somewhat misleading because there's no hint of domesticating Jesus to fit a personal agenda. The Christ consciousness that emerges in Gabrielle reveals a soul who is inspired for all of us. Through her love of our Lord, she transformed her life and living for universal benefits and coparticipation in redemption for all humankind.

The path of colloquy is one of love, surrender, humility, and devotion. Often when we are attracted to colloquy we also use music, song, and affective melodies, chants, and ceaseless repetition of the name of the Beloved. When praying, we would have a specific image of our Lord and give our total attention to Christ who is our teacher, friend, spouse, our Beloved. The self-talk is silent when union abides.

This practice of colloquy came naturally with me. After years and years of colloquy with our Lord, there was a shift following that sustained *lectio* on the Holy Spirit. This colloquy is quieter, more subtle communication with, from, and to the Holy Spirit. There's also no choice on my part whom I talk to. Trinity is one and I bring my little thoughts to the God who is so very present in the Presence.

Since this book is about discernment and the personal presence of the Holy Spirit, I am sure the invitation to colloquy with the Holy Spirit is offered to souls like mine. The Holy Spirit is an entity, so there's proper dialogue with this Person. My aunt Arlene Funk had this relationship and she was holy. Her devotion spilled into her everyday relationships. She saw the Holy Spirit at work everywhere and within everyone.

The practice of colloquy is to remember that there's no point in talking to oneself as our Lord gave us this Spirit who forgives sins and who abides in us. Because of Jesus Christ's humanity, all humans are joined to the Trinity. This Son of the Father, Jesus Christ, breathed on us the Holy Spirit. We—Father, Son, Spirit, us—include but are more than all created matter; we are inextricably connected.

The Little Way of Thérèse of Lisieux: The Method of the Little Way as Taught by Thérèse of Lisieux

Thérèse of the Holy Child Jesus was born Marie Françoise Thérèse Martin in 1873 in Alençon, France, into an intensely devout family, which nurtured her profound spiritual awareness. Thérèse's mother died when she was four yours old, and for the next eight years she struggled with an overly sensitive and timid nature.

On Christmas Day 1886, before her fourteenth birthday, she was released from her emotional weakness and received the gift of "love and a spirit of self-forgetfulness." Thereafter, she prepared to become a Carmelite and obtained hard-won permission to enter the Lisieux Carmel at the age of fifteen.

Rejecting the extreme penances common at this time, Thérèse practiced unspectacular self-denial, recognizing that everyday events have spiritual value. Her final illness and death in 1897 at the age of twenty-four was marked by physical suffering and excruciating spiritual darkness, which she endured for the sake of souls who had no faith.

She wrote fifty-four poems. Her autobiography, *The Story of a Soul*, is a compilation of three manuscripts written from 1873 to 1897. In it she describes her Little Way of recognizing our nothingness and offering the depths of our poverty to God emotion by emotion in a practice that is conscious and actual, expecting everything from God and trusting in God's merciful love.

The Little Way is offering our very self to merciful love. We need not be perfect. It is sufficient to present ourselves to God as we are. The depth of God's mercy is attracted to the depth of our poverty. Instead of relying on our own spiritual accomplishments, we must rely only on the strength of Jesus.

This is a way of faith. Eternal life to those who believe is the promise of Jesus. Our responsibility is to believe that this is true and live our lives accordingly.

The gospel events have energy to sustain us in this pursuit of the ordinary way, the Little Way of being a person. God rewards littleness if we bear with ourselves along with our imperfections. The Little Way is a short, quick, straight way, an urgent need to fulfill our desire to be one with God. "Let the little children come to me; do not stop them" (Mark 10:14).

The Little Way is premised on an image of a mother holding a child. The arms of Jesus lift the child up to the mother. The smaller you are, the easier it is to lift you up. The gift of littleness is that we become light, not weighed down by anxiety, guilt, dread, and heaviness.

Littleness cuts the bonds that drag us down. When we are little, we expect everything from God. We let go of anxiety, fear, and self-centeredness and rely only on God. We have nothing. God is all. So we own, accept, and face our nothingness. The "little" part of the Little Way is all about nothingness. The "way" part is about renouncing attachment to emotions or feelings. Even when my desires are dried up, this ache after God is part of the littleness that I experience.

Yes, this is duality (not dualism that separates with judgment), the experience of being creature with God as Creator. Through Christ Jesus the soul advances into the human Christ and becomes one, but the starting point is other.

In *lectio* with St. Thérèse's writings, I learned that she was like her teacher, St. John of the Cross, *apophatic* to the core. There are no revelations or apparitions of Christ

Jesus or other saints. This is raw faith, and instead of using words for prayer, she lifts up her feelings, desires, and emotions as if they were a prayer. Her simple, ordinary life was toward God instant by instant, feeling by feeling, and prick by prick. She refrained from feeling sorry for herself; in fact, she refrained from going up the chain of feelings and into the self-talk of being wounded and hurt. She offered her emotional life to God and returned all feelings of love in faith toward God.

So, the "way" in the Little Way was all about renouncing emotional self-talk and giving all love to God. A welcome feature of the Little Way is that there is no disdain of creatures. Rather, loving God enabled her to love much. Nothingness was a brilliant way to restrain herself from any illusions, any false expectations of a return on emotional investment. To get at the uniqueness of this path, we only have to think of the brilliance of St. John of the Cross renouncing all thought of God in prayer and undergoing the dark nights to let God be God in his soul.

In St. Thérèse we have a renunciation of self-centered affect. She would say of herself that she never let herself take a vacation from giving all. To preempt the question of repressed emotions, it is clear that in her nothingness she already dealt with anger, depression, and the drag of the human condition. She understood that she was really and truly nothing. Therefore, for her to renounce emotions would simply be to embrace truth. She had no ego consciousness to nurture. She literally preferred nothing to Christ.

How did she reach such heights? She was a super-sensitive child, having lost her mother at age four and having episodes of separation anxiety. She had an extraordinary grace when she was almost fourteen years old. She instantly grew up on Christmas Eve 1886 at the words of her father that pierced her to the heart. From that night, she says of herself that she no longer wanted to live for herself but to substitute her life for another's.

This was her prayer when she prayed for the conversion of Pranzini, a man being executed for murder. For her, faith was seamless. Ask and it shall be given, even if it were the salvation of a sinner. All will be granted through God's mercy.

Suffering for her was the way to transmute desire. Her desire was only one thing: always to suffer for Jesus. It is through suffering that we can save souls, and these souls praise God for all eternity. Suffering and adoration, then, were the same act.

We know that in this Little Way Thérèse had genuine love and affection for others. She was not worried over the growing affection she felt for her novice mistress. The friendship that united them was very pure and could only help them in their desire to love God above all else. Her relationships were well ordered since she loved God above any human being and she loved others through God's love.

She gave her daily actions to God, working without hurry to stay in the present moment. She refused nothing if it were given to her. She learned to prefer whatever happened. In her focus on God's mercy, she offered her littleness and nothingness to God.

Through the discipline of giving her all (her nothingness without the illusion of being anything) she practiced loving others without reserve. This quick way was a surrender in faith of all return on her affect. Her sacrifice was to take the same delight in the difficult nuns as in the winsome ones. We might even say it was a "way of affect," to give whatever she felt to God.

She was tested with aridity, feeling nothing, but she continued to act as if all was a joy for her. And she says of herself that she was indeed very happy in spite of much suffering. Her surrender gave way to gratitude. Profound peace characterizes her writings. There's nothing childlike about her words; they illustrate a mature, full-bodied love. In her Little Way, she renounced her self-centered self.

Everything she did was a ritual rather than simply a function. When she served as sacristan, filling the ciborium with hosts was a priestly act, but it was also an expression of her apostolate of filling heaven with souls. She painted and wrote poetry and prose, accomplishing each task without becoming seduced by it.

Her goal was not to be successful by making a public impression. She felt that our work should not hinder our praying. Our time should be used consciously but with a detached heart. If we discover new imperfections in ourselves, we do something about it. Disappointments only motivate us to strive. Love like a child but fight like

Joan of Arc. God calls us all to holiness. If we are called to the Little Way, we should practice it without desiring ecstasies or warm consolations. The Little Way is an *apophatic* way, a way of faith.

We should desire not to do outstanding works but to be invisible. This is a practice of virtue so hidden that the left hand doesn't know what the right hand is doing. It requires us to renounce ourselves, honor others, and be of service. We must be detached from results, let go of our needs and considerations.

To be a servant or a slave, subject to the whims and wishes of another, reverses our tendency toward self-love. God becomes visible through others. We let ourselves be found, loved, and fashioned by God. God always loves us first. We are little, empty. The practice asks us to keep empty so we can receive. We respond by loving others ahead of ourselves. In this Little Way, we let ourselves be carried, empty handed, devoid of all merit, absolutely embraced gratuitously. God's love for us we see in faith, and we demonstrate our love for God in service and sacrifice toward others. We please God rather than merit affection from others.

Thérèse wanted to be completely immersed in the fire of Love and offer herself to merciful Love. She saw herself as a "victim, even a holocaust," consumed by the fire of Divine Love. This desire was a testimony that her deepest happiness was in being tested and found faithful.

She did not see annihilation as a goal. Her goal was full immersion in and merging with Divine Love. Though she is sometimes perceived as childlike, she fully embraced suffering. Feminine in tone, she preferred the path of accepting the ordinary rather than the path of miracles, visions, and heroic mortifications.

When we pray, as we practice the Little Way, we think about God and do free association, renouncing all that is not God. The path is one of faith, dark faith, with no content except faith. We join Jesus in the gospels. Experiencing aridity, nothingness, no thought, and no return on our efforts are to be expected. Prayers, reading, and devotions are difficult if not impossible at this stage.

For Thérèse, prayer was a movement of the heart, a simple gaze toward heaven, a cry of gratitude and love in the midst of trial as well as joy. Nevertheless, she did not recite prayers in common without devotion. On the contrary, she loved common prayer because Jesus promised to be in the midst of those who gather in his name. Sometimes, if she could not concentrate on the mysteries of the rosary, she wrote them down or prayed the Hail Mary very slowly. Prayer was not easy for her, but it was essential.

Once she renounced deep silence during a retreat to talk to Sister Martha who was hurting. Her general confession was helpful to St. Thérèse. It helped her put her tendency to scrupulosity behind her. She never looked back after that confession.

She used flowers as an idiom for how she saw beauty in the various things, events, and people in her path. Each thing was used for good, for beauty. St. Thérèse chose all and did all for God. Nothing was wasted.

Nothing was too small. The "little" in her Little Way meant that everything is a means. Nothing is omitted and all is done in love.

Her asceticism is rigorous in its totality and comprehensiveness. Her amazing effort is to be empty so that God is all. She allowed no escape for herself. She took no vacations from this ascetic path.

God calls all of us to holiness. We learn from St. Thérèse that the Little Way is without ecstasies or spiritual presence. It is hidden. She let God be God, allowing God to find her, love her, fashion her. She never exalted her gifts and wrote her story only under obedience. Her practice was laying aside anything for herself in her emotional life of feelings. She suffered willingly and offered her well-being as a sacrifice for the well-being of others.

Her genius goes on to teach us more: all little acts of self-surrender can be used for substitutive suffering. We suffer and can use our suffering so that someone else does not have to suffer. We actually prevent suffering for someone else because we do it for them. In this exchange, all in faith lifting our hearts toward the All Merciful Love of Jesus who has redeemed us all, we join in his merits and in faith know that this actually heals and transforms others. Again, this is all faith and is steeped in the Christian biblical sensitivities of the nature of sacrifice having been fully satisfied by the cross and resurrection of Christ Jesus.

This is the good news. Suffering has meaning and can be transmuted to help others. Our little saint, Thérèse, gives us concrete teachings. What is more exceptional is that she promises to come with her teachings. She is a patron saint that is spending her heaven doing good through us. We no longer need to pick up a life of prayer and sacrifice; we use our ordinary emotions and ride our faith upon those flowers of intention.

There is story after story of conversions. Many priests and sinners attribute their new life of apostolic love to some connection with St. Thérèse. Her Little Way of using ordinary consciousness of feelings and relationships is prayer. It is a practice that becomes prayer when made into one's way of life. Prayer is lifting up the heart to God. So, how do we do this? An example is the situation of having to drive in slow, halting traffic with impetuous drivers riding too close behind:

- I notice the irritation rising in my emotions.

- I offer this discomfort to God.

- I offer without any hesitation because I am little and this is the way of praying.

- I offer for the sake of ———. (Here, I place an intention.)

- I suffer so that someone will not have to suffer.

- I join my sufferings in faith to the redemptive suffering of Jesus on the cross.

- I do this as many times as I notice my feeling of emotional stress.

We are attracted to the Little Way because this path helps us to recognize our nothingness, to expect everything from God, as a child expects everything from its father or mother.

We feel incapable of earning eternal life. St. Thérèse shows us, however, that, like a child, we should simply pick flowers, the flowers of love and sacrifice, and offer them to God for his pleasure, doing very little things with great love. Each petal (little sufferings) offered to Jesus is small, but, through offering, our little sufferings transmute emotional pain into sacrifice joined to Christ for the sake of all humankind.

The Little Way is profound. This is a path of sorting through our particular moments of emotional troubles and using that very stuff of life as prayer and a skillful means of substituting our loss for another's gain. Thérèse loved suffering. I don't, as yet, love suffering, but I do know that through my own tests and trials this practice can determine how I can help deal with suffering. There's a fine line between healthy suffering and a sick kind of attraction to suffering. This is not in the spirit of the Little Flower. She suffered what was *given*; she actually renounced the ascetical ways of doing suffering for Jesus that came from one's own agenda. Her point is that when suffering comes our way, we embrace it and use it to help others. The passive suffering of living with pain is sometimes accompanied with an active life doing selfless service for others. Her genius and her work from the other side not only teach her Little Way but help us do it. This saint is working on our behalf. I've heard story after story of great gifts given when asked that are attributed to her intercession.

The Jesus Prayer/Prayer of the Heart: The Practice of Ceaseless Prayer in the Christian Tradition

This is the traditional practice of ceaseless prayer in the Christian tradition. If we are to listen to the Holy Spirit and discern with the ear of our hearts, we must first find our hearts. For myself, I lived for years and years in my head. I felt no capacity to discern, placing my mind in my heart. The practice of the Jesus Prayer is for those who want to descend their minds into their heart. What is the tradition of the Jesus Prayer?

The Jesus Prayer: "Jesus, Son of God, Have mercy on me, a sinner." The long form is, "Jesus, Son of the Living God, have mercy on me, a sinner." Shorter forms include, "Jesus, have mercy on me," or, "Jesus, mercy," or, "*Kyrie, eleison*." The shortest form is simply, "Jesus."

When it is practiced over time, it drops to the heart and becomes the prayer of the heart. The teachings are rich: The invocation of the Holy Name of Jesus, which continues our baptismal immersion, brings our attention to Christ, and Christ, in turn, dwells in us.

The prayer warms the heart and becomes an experience of Presence. In the Christian East a *staretz* would caution the pilgrim that it takes assiduous practice. But with some years of practice, the Jesus Prayer can become ceaseless and self-acting.

The training for the method of the Jesus Prayer has three stages:

1. making of the habit or physically committing the prayer to memory
2. virtual or mental spontaneous prayer that rises from time to time
3. actual or self-acting continuous prayer

To make it habitual, we are to say the words (invocation) of the prayer slowly, mindfully, and with respect for the meaning of the words. This is practiced at specific times with a certain number, like using one's rosary to do fifty prayers in five sets. Rest and do another fifty times in five sets. Do this morning and evening for two weeks. Then increase it to one hundred times in ten sets morning and night. After a couple of months, add another set midday of one hundred repetitions in ten sets.

Notice I didn't use the word "sit." The Jesus Prayer is a "working" prayer, done as we do other things. It's not a meditation practice like centering prayer.

Keep increasing gradually until you start to feel the prayer rising automatically in between times. If for some reason the practice is stopped, start again and make it easy to start with the sets of fifty repetitions. After about two months (sometimes I've known people who have passed the first stage in two weeks), it becomes ceaseless prayer; the Jesus Prayer will be self-acting and going on all the time.

The next stage is virtual. The prayer continues for several months or even years but in adversity or lack of mindfulness it drops from consciousness. This is because the habit was only virtual, not actual. We simply start again and do the strenuous effort to make it a habit again. Usually, the second or third time it is easier.

Often when we are in a period of an affliction, when we need the prayer most of all, it goes away. It simply must be brought to the afflictive thought of food, sex, anger, and so on. In practice, the Jesus Prayer goes on continually, but more especially so when we are challenged with a temptation or an inclination away from our resolve.

The final stage is actual. The Jesus Prayer actually is praying itself! I do not know of anyone in this stage because while we are in this life we must always be vigilant that our prayer be constant. We can fall away anytime, but God's grace is stronger. And this prayer has no anxiety attached to it. When or if it stops, we simply and gently start again, and it returns to its place in our consciousness.

Jesus Prayer becomes a Breath Prayer. Sometimes the Jesus Prayer is called The Breath Prayer since it is in sync with one's breath: We inhale saying "Lord, Jesus Christ," then pause, saying mentally, "Son of the Living God," and then exhale, saying, "have mercy on me, a sinner." Eventually the words have a cadence that is automatic and starts to follow our breath.

With practice, the breath itself becomes the prayer without words. The breath carries our intention. In English, the formula is long so some find it easier to shorten the formula to "Jesus, mercy," or, "*Kyrie, Eleison*." The repetition should be done slowly, softly, and quietly. Gentle, like a feather, since this is anointing the soul and celebrating the Presence.

Jesus Prayer moves through the breath to the heart. The Jesus Prayer evolves from the lips to the mind through the breath to the heart and becomes the prayer of the heart. This third phase is more of a gift than an intentional effort. It usually happens on retreat or in times of protracted quiet.

The prayer of the heart is to find that place in the heart where "rest" happens. Contemplative prayer is beyond thought. Even though it's usually a by-product of the Jesus Prayer, once we've experienced the prayer of the heart, we can descend to that place at will.

This traditional practice is to descend the mind in the heart and give attention to the heartbeat that carries the intent of the Jesus Prayer. In Eastern Christianity this is practiced while gazing at an icon. Our gaze descends to our heart while we practice faith that God is gazing at us. Our mind's eye is in the physical/spiritual heart.

It is important to know that if we accompany the Jesus Prayer with breath or heartbeat in prolonged periods during an intensive sitting method, we need a spiritual director or an elder who has this practice. This practice is so powerful that our life takes on a more demanding spiritual sensitivity.

We rededicated ourselves to guard of the heart and watchfulness of thoughts with the memory of Jesus whom we are experiencing in our very being. So the companion practice in ordinary waking consciousness is the guard of the heart.

The teachings continue to say that the prayer of the heart is practiced ceaselessly as was the Jesus Prayer, but instead of mentally saying the invocation of the name, there is the practice of warming the heart with love.

The Jesus Prayer/prayer of the heart is assisted by using a rosary (or prayer rope) so that the person can physically use the whole body, when walking, when waiting, or during designated prayer periods. The Jesus Prayer is portable and is meant to be done in all one's waking time. It is most helpful to do upon waking and before sleep. Even when we are in our first training we need not "sit" and meditate on it.

One can do it while walking, waiting, or doing dishes. It's an active prayer. Some teach that in initial stages, it is helpful to concentrate and dedicate a few minutes, like ten minutes here and there, to say the Jesus Prayer with full attention. But I find that if folks wait for reordering their life to get those ten minutes of attention together, they never get started.

So just start where you are with whatever you are doing. It is especially friendly to do during manual labor that is repetitive and doesn't need your whole attention.

Some people worry that if they do the Jesus Prayer their "leftover" mind for attentive work, like computer, teaching, or social work, will be too occupied. When the mind needs to be attentive to "other work," the Jesus Prayer will drop down in consciousness, and the brain will activate a clear mental process for the business at hand.

The benefit of the Jesus Prayer is that, while one is doing manual or mental work, one is more attentive since the prayer is "at work" reducing unwanted distractions and aiding one's concentration. The yanking into consciousness of the eight thoughts is reduced. The mind is at peace. This actually frees the conscious mind to be more receptive to whomever you are listening.

The fruit of the Jesus Prayer is that it becomes the prayer of the heart and an abiding presence of God. This Presence is usually *apophatic*, without image. Yet there is an experience of the Presence that you feel with your spiritual senses.

The Jesus Prayer does not replace other forms of prayer such as Divine Office, Liturgy of the Eucharist, or *lectio divina*. It is, however, the unifying prayer that brings to life the other prayer forms that are part of our specific vocation.

Even in dryness the Jesus Prayer has no heaviness, no languishing, no struggling. It has a life of its own that is an experience of profound peace felt by the spiritual senses, the eyes of the soul. Instead of aridity, the feeling of compunction rises. This is the twin feeling of being so loved by, so close to, God but also so vastly separated by littleness and even sin. This double emotion is charged with desire that is so deep that no other satisfaction can penetrate this deeply felt abiding consciousness. The words of the Jesus Prayer and the ongoing disposition of *penthos* prevent dejection, vainglory, and pride. We keep our heart listening like a boat coming in to safe harbor.

Can everyone do it? While everyone can do this prayer, not everyone is called to it. We know we are called to it if these four conditions are present:

1. we feel drawn toward the invocation of the Name
2. we see that the practice produces in us an increase of charity, purity, obedience, and peace
3. we find the use of other prayer practices become somewhat difficult
4. finally, we find that the Jesus Prayer simplifies our life and provides a unity to our spiritual life

The practice of the Jesus Prayer will thrive unless one sins. When (notice, I'm not saying "if" because the human condition continues in each one of us) sin happens, simply return to the practice immediately without hesitation. Resume the practice, and it will be an aid to resist temptation in the future.

The request for mercy is real. *Penthos* is an abiding state of remaining "in the need of God's mercy." With spiritual practices comes a clear, focused mind that can leap to vainglory without the sense of being "in need of God." Radically, to the core, one feels the need of help.

This is a sense of *penthos* or compunction because of being a sinner.[13]

A fuller explanation and teaching about this tradition of the Jesus Prayer is present in the Christian East, especially in the writings of the *Philokalia*. The Jesus Prayer is rooted in Scripture. We can accompany our practice with *lectio* on the Scripture passages that recommend it.

The dominant fruit of this practice of the Jesus Prayer that becomes prayer of the heart is that moment, place, and space of contemplation experienced by each of us. A profound silence brings together our fragmented mind, and we become stable and attentive. After years of practice, one can descend the mind into the heart at will and find that place of stillness (*hesychia*).

To hear the still, small, as-if voice of the Holy Spirit, we must be calm and awake. The Jesus Prayer is the practice of choice for many contemplatives in the monastic tradition. The invitation rises through a graced moment when the Holy Name of Jesus joins again with those early baptismal waters in the soul. We are overshadowed and re-created once again. This time, through the ceaseless practice of the Jesus Prayer, those waters never evaporate. The Holy Spirit confirms the presence of God in our soul.

Breakpoints When the Ascetical Practice Becomes Prayer

There are break points in the practices that become prayer. Consciousness is restructured: Formerly, we were in our thinking mind, talking to ourselves. After this shift, we know God from our own experience, and if there is talk at all, it is shared presence with the Presence. We undergo prayer. It happens *to* us. This is the mystical voice heard by the spiritual senses. Here are the break points in practices named in the text above.

The Practice of the Presence

When moment by moment we stop our work, pray, and listen to God in the present moment, it soon becomes a habit. The practice then shifts from saying words, lifting up one's heart in prayer, to profound awareness of the present moment. Now is God. Instead of moments strung together in sequential time, the point of realization awakens and expands from chronological time. The moment is God. God's presence in spaciousness and mystery happens in actuality. This praying often in the Presence takes on a shift so that one feels the presence of God. This mystical moment expands to a glow that feels like being in love and in a universal experience of God consciousness. The shift is from moment of present prayers to a Presence.

It is similar to striking a match. At first there are a few sparks, but then the final strike ignites the flame. We practice and practice; then, at a moment in time, with the grace of God, the friction causes the fire.

The warm energy of being in the undifferentiated Presence is personal and abiding. There comes a second mystical moment that requires deeper and gentler receptivity. The mystical moment becomes an experience of faith in the Presence. This is more like adoration or ritual worship inversing all matter as holy. It's more mature and less emotional to feel this abiding faith in the Presence, but it cleans out the subtle temptation to be in one's own presence and light and not completely prostrate before the Holy Other.

The Practice of Self-Abandonment to the Present Moment

This practice is to accept actively and passively the necessity of the present moment. What is is. We see God's will in the moment that is given. Our faith tells us that all is by God's design. We do our duty. We neither pine for the past nor live in a fantasy of the future. We see our state in life as our vocation, and God is now and active in our moments of time. We structure our time, relationships, work, and prayers to conform more and more to the will of God. We do things for God, with God, and in God.

The practice shifts dramatically after a break point: at a point in the practice the necessity and duty become so interior that we do only the will of God. We are like a clay pot that has been broken and stashed in the corner. From time to time God brings us out for the moment; we function and then are tossed unnoticed in the corner, awaiting our next directive. We now experience God in us doing the work. We no longer live, but Christ lives in us.

The Practice of the Cloud of Unknowing

At first, a single-syllable word such as "love" is used time and time again, piercing the unknowing realm with that steady intent to love and forget all else. The practice purifies the psyche of thoughts that are not of God. This sweet obsession becomes a habit: to signal love toward "that God is" and to simply accept the oneness of being "that I am." There is a peace in such sheer immediacy with God, and nothing else is active and conscious in the mind.

The shift happens when that being-to-being connection is felt existentially. The heart knows.

The Practice of Recollection

St. Teresa of Avila had major mystical revelations and still she went back to her mindlessness and divided heart. Finally, after her definitive revelation, she prayed to the Holy Spirit for a sustained grace to stay faithful to Christ our Lord Jesus as the direct and only center of her heart. She practiced and taught that it is not enough to know Jesus in big moments; we need to practice staying focused and aware of Jesus being specifically in this room with these people during this conversation or this work.

Recollection is a practice of faith that at first is a major effort just to remember that God is present. This practice takes weeks of intense concentration, but then the memory relaxes into the reality that Jesus is indeed present, and the mind no longer resists the intrusion of faith overriding ordinary senses.

The shift happens that soon, and very soon, the mind finds a very quiet and still place. This effort at recollection becomes prayer of quiet. The representing of Jesus in the situations of ordinary consciousness is no longer necessary. No image is needed.

The Practice of Colloquy: Dialogue with Our Lord

The practice is to watch that inner talk that usually refers to the self. We shift self-talk to talking to our Lord. At first, it happens some of the time, then most of the time. If our Lord is present, then it seems natural to share that experience through this inner dialogue. Over time, the dialogue has a life of its own. It is as if we hear Jesus and as if we are talking to him out loud. Sometimes Jesus starts the conversation and sometimes we start it, but soon it becomes familiar and very real. There is a shared awareness like friends know or lovers enjoy.

The practice shifts from intermittent dialogue and episodic sound bites to less talk and a never-not-shared consciousness together. While there is no merging, as we remain creatures before the Creator, the sweetness of abiding is a steady state. The Holy Spirit abides.

The Little Way of Thérèse of Lisieux

The early stage is to notice emotional or physical suffering and to use it as prayer. Noticing that being "little" and "not much" is the way it is and God's merciful love can use my personal suffering for showering redemptive love on others. The practice is to lift up the suffering often and in a childlike manner with candor and raw expectation that my prayers will be answered. The ordinary stuff of inner afflictions replaces the outer, outmoded, contrived sacrifices of mortification.

The shift is profound: suffering is loved because it is a way to love God with one's whole heart and soul and to love others more than oneself. It is an immersion in the "I thirst" of Jesus on the cross. We live in the wounds of Christ.

The Jesus Prayer/Prayer of the Heart

For the first couple of years, there is a ceaseless prayer that rises with little or no effort. The mantra is soft and available for comfort and mindfulness. The steady stream of the words fades to softer-than-soft background music but is always heard when tuned in. It seems that when the Jesus Prayer continues ever deeper and steadier the breathing and cadence of the words merge. Then the break point happens: the prayer simply drops down into the heart. It is mostly self-acting and the mind's eye finds great comfort in resting in the heart.

In prayer of the heart, the prayer descends into the heart. So the "door" is not to take words and consciously point them to the heart but to allow the mind to descend. The mind here is the *nous*—a Greek word that simply doesn't translate well into English. It means the "mind in the heart" or consciousness that resides in the body.

So the break point happens when praying—saying the prayer and making it a habit. It then becomes a prayer with its own life stream, praying through the body and mind and resting in the soul. In the first phase *we* pray. The break point shifts to the actual experience of God dwelling in our hearts. God is praying *in* us rather than us praying to God.

Cautions at This Stage in the Practice

Each of these prayer practices is sturdy, effective, and blessed by saints and holy ones who have gone before us. Nevertheless, being human, we can be deceived. A wise elder can detect when self-absorption is activated, when someone is seduced by a charismatic personality, when one is overly identified with the thinking mind. But most of all, a wise elder can detect if the seeker is ready and seeking self-honesty without flattery. Delusional personalities tend to attract each other. As to how to find a wise elder, we must rely on the Holy Spirit. Humility would be a required criteria. Humility is what others see when someone has purity of heart.

In each of the practices, there's a prerequisite to be repentant and confess sin. The cause of breakdown sometimes happens when one strives too hard to be virtuous while simultaneously going the opposite direction in one's moral life.

In addiction counseling, I've heard of counselors recommending a mantric prayer to replace the addictive thought (food, drink, sex, things, anger, depression, etc.). The repetition of the prayer, like that which is done in the Jesus Prayer, is too strong for someone just starting to get his or her life together. Meditation practices require humility. We must wait upon grace to discern how, when, where, and what to pray.

The brain sometimes copes by morphing into an alternative universe if the person simply shifts into a ceaseless mantra without help to overcome the addictive behavior. Meditation alters the chemistry of the brain, and if the brain has been compromised by chemical dependencies, it is best to use softer and milder techniques to overcome the afflictive thoughts. The substitute of ceaseless prayer is simply too high of an antidote. The person needs to start with colloquy or recollection.

Meditation practice can be helpful if the person has *not* been on drugs and mind-altering techniques. What I recommend for recovering addicts is that, instead of meditation, they do manual labor and dialogue with a friend with honesty and accountability. Persons in active addictions need the services of local programs. There is a danger of spiritualizing ordinary failures and human hubris. Discernment sorts out the source of the problem as well as the treatment and ongoing prevention of sin and suffering. Humility is ground zero.

We never consider ourselves beyond the eight afflictive thoughts. While these afflictions can be extirpated, we always know our vulnerability. Circumstances, weak moments, and compromised situations can strut out our former demons or engage us with brand new temptations.

How do we make those decisions? We turn now to ways of making choices through the doors of discernment.

Chapter 3

Specific Practices for Discernment

We need to learn how to make decisions through discernment. This means to explicitly ask the Holy Spirit what to do, how to do it, and what the expectations are for taking action. This asking does not mean to skip doing homework. Discernment is an engaging process that takes time, energy, and stamina. Over the years these five steps have proven to be helpful as a method. This process is designed for big decisions but also very helpful for little choices that come my way every day, like what should be my Lenten book? Or do I offer to take sister's phone duty? Or do I write that book review?

Five Steps to Making a Decision

I have many opportunities to choose between this and that. I have invitations or circumstances that cut off possibilities. Changes are inevitable. My risk-to-benefit ratio can be large or small, but my little choices make all the difference. My desire is God, so how do I follow my heart's desire? We take care and attention to move in the direction of God's will for us. This is the way of discernment: to make a decision is using our faith and ability to choose wisely.

Step 1: We Ask the Holy Spirit to Help

What is the question before me? Sometimes we ask for the right answer but fail to ask the right question. It's important to ask the Holy Spirit this question: "What is before me?" The practice of holy indifference starts here with the *question* so that both the question and the directive (answer) are sorted out toward my vocation of seeking God. What does God want of me here? What is the choice before me? It's more about observing than thinking. I watch and see what rises. This pause, this asking before acting, requires spiritual poise. This first step is to ask myself what I should be asking of the Holy Spirit.

I invoke the Holy Spirit to come: Help me decide to make the right choice on this matter. In the introduction text, we had a short teaching on the prayer form of *epiclesis*. In this five-step process, the point is to do it. We use our ordinary words and our own voice. There is no one else who can do this for us. The cry for help has to come from our own heart!

Step 2: Make a Virtual Decision

We take a tentative answer that seems to be the most likely solution or plausible way of moving forward on this matter. We make a virtual decision as if it were the way we were going to proceed. Notice the word "virtual." This is done in our minds. We do not have to act out all the options, seek advice, or do analytical research. We have the moment of grace within us. We can trust that if we need more information or if we don't know what to do the next step will be revealed to us. In this virtual reality we sort our thoughts.

We refrain from thinking. Instead, we observe our thoughts that rise. At first it seems random; then, we see a pattern that can be sorted in four categories:

- thoughts from God
- thoughts from self
- thoughts from others
- thoughts from evil forces

The sorting continues: sort feelings, images, scenarios, and consequences—yet, not from the thinking mind, but from the observing eye that watches how the thoughts are sourced and the direction they are going. Some are from God going to God, some from the self going to self, some from others going to others, some from evil going to evil. If we have trouble keeping our minds focused, we can write notes on paper, sorting the thoughts into the four categories.

If nothing rises pertaining to the question, we might check if we have the right question and affirm our virtual option. Most of the time, when this happens we just need more silence and calming techniques. Our attention is scattered, but our mind will gradually inform our consciousness. This decision-making process simply demonstrates the importance of knowing our thoughts and that thoughts are a skillful means of knowing.

Step 3: Ask for a Confirming Sign

I prefer to live into the option that comes from God. I see the strength of the virtual decision. I ask for a confirming sign that if I take action on this option it will be God's will for me.

- A confirming sign has the indicators of being good for me.

- The sign comes from the outside (not my idea).

- The sign pertains to the question at hand. There's a link, a connection that I can see.

- The action I need to take has an accompanying grace to make it possible, even if it is difficult and requires some suffering.

- It is big, or at least in proportion to the gravity of the decision. It rules out doubt.

If there is no confirming sign, I go back to step 2 and take another alternative action to the question under consideration. Then, I repeat step 3. I do this as many times as it takes to get a confirming sign.

This process takes time. We need time and silence to calm down our thinking mind and shift into observation of our thoughts. This is vigilance, a watching. If we do this interior work, we'll not make mistakes in our external actions that take days, weeks, and years to remediate and mend.

Notice that during this virtual process we do not do data gathering by asking others their opinion. They will only tell us what they would do in our situation. That is not helpful, unless it is our married partner or our religious superior. When we have too many voices between our ears, the result is confusion. If more data is necessary, that will be the next step of this process. For now, observe thoughts. The answer is usually already in one's heart.

The question here is what God wants me to do. This is discernment, not management. If we need more facts or pertinent data, that thought will rise and with it will come the appropriate source for that information. Usually, these decisions are not statistically verifiable but more personally appropriate for our lives as a whole. This is closer to insight than to logic. Discernment is to see the parts in light of the whole.

Step 4: Make the Decision

We accept the confirming sign and we make the decision. This decision sets the direction. This way forward cuts off options at this time. Action must be taken because the process of deliberation is completed. We ritualize the decision with a signature on a deed, a down payment on a car, marking our calendar, lighting a candle, or taking a walk to the shore. This ritual is something to set the decision in a specific time and place and to be remembered as finalized with closure. Then, we take the action required.

Step 5: Watch Thoughts and Guard Heart

From time to time there will be difficulties and second thoughts of doubt, distance, and recalculating the risks involved that offset the benefits. This is the time to watch our thoughts and guard our hearts. We put the decision in a box with boundaries around the dimensions.

We stay firm and do not open the decision for reconsideration. This is a temptation, not an invitation. If God wants something else, it will happen to us; we do not have to initiate it. We rest confidently in the knowledge that we asked for the right question and then prayed to the Holy Spirit. We watched our thoughts and waited on the guidance that comes through our thoughts, feelings, and images. We respectfully waited on the Holy Spirit for a confirming sign and then made the decision. If, for some reason, it is wrong, that is not our problem; we did all in good faith, and the right direction will flow from our good hearts and complete faith. We are confident that God cares about the little and big choices in our lives and will reveal the directives to us. This is discernment.

To change habits we first must be willing to unlearn destructive patterns and then practice the new ones. Without the follow through to act into the decision there is no virtue (habit of doing good). Sometimes we do not take care enough to do the necessary work that it takes to hear and heed the directives of the Holy Spirit. It seems daunting, but the same Spirit that directs our heart can also move us to change our habits.

The fruits of the Spirit are love, joy, peace, patience, kindness, goodness, faithfulness, gentleness, and self-control (Gal 5:22-23a). In Paul's Letter to the Romans, he tells us that the Spirit aids us in our weakness: "for we do not know how to pray as we ought, but that very Spirit intercedes with sighs too deep for words" (8:26). And the Spirit intercedes for all the holy ones according to God's will. We know that "all things work together for good for those who love God" (Rom 8:28).

The five-step method works well when there's a clear question and a preferred answer. But another method is story. We simply ask ourselves, "What's the story here?" In the telling of the story, the way of God, who is our heart's desire, emerges with clarity and grace.

Three Examples of Discernment

Like all practices, there is no other way of learning them except by doing them. To know about discernment or moral consciousness is better after one has had the experience. Hence, we need to start now with little decisions so we are ready to discern major directions in our vocation.

Example 1: Speculative Reading *or* Lectio Divina*?*

This was the situation: at the Daughters of Charity Retreat Center, Mater Dei, near Evansville, Indiana, I checked out of their library Karen Armstrong's book *A Case for God*, a 432-page paperback.

Question: Is God asking me to renounce reading speculative theology and philosophy in the Christian or Eastern traditions? Is this book for me? Is it *lectio* or just one more book? Next, I went through the five-step process to discern if reading this book is God's will for me.

Step 1: Ask the question. Is this the right question? Would renouncing speculative reading be what God wants of me? If I am doing some outreach, I may need to study a book that comes my way that is helpful for my ministry. But I'm asking the question about *lectio*. Do I read book after book instead of doing *lectio* deeply and in a sustained manner? Do I take eight hours and read this book?

I pray an *epiclesis*:

> Come, Holy Spirit, come.
> Bring to mind your grace
> to see God's way for me.
> Come, Holy Spirit, come.

Step 2: Make an as-if decision and sort thoughts. I enjoy speculative reading and thinking. I read the introduction and sorted through the chapters—maybe forty minutes of just holding and moving through the book, trying to decide if I was going to take the week to read it while I was in Evansville or maybe ask the librarian at Beech Grove to acquire it.

I framed the virtual decision that no, I was not going to read it and then went on to breakfast, prayers, and give my first retreat presentation. I watched my thoughts and sorted them:

From self: Karen Armstrong has been a good teacher for me in interfaith dialogue. She writes so clearly. Brilliant mind. I could use her thinking when I'm asked questions as I lecture, write, and converse.

From God: Would more thoughts about God help me know God? Would my silence be filled with more thinking? When have I read enough? Don't I already know the gist of the arguments about God?

From others: I'll look smarter if I can remember Karen Armstrong's careful constructs. I should keep up in my field.

From evil: I can outsmart those who challenge me, especially those who don't know as much as I do.

Step 3: Confirming sign. A confirming sign came to me: I received an email from a university asking me to teach a course in the coming year. I felt keenly that academic settings belong to my former way of life. Not now. I've been a nun fifty years and am just beginning to live in my cell. No time to teach graduate students about God. I need to know God myself.

Step 4: Make the decision. The decision is no, I won't read this book. I ritualized the decision by taking the book back to the library.

Step 5: Prevent relapse into taking back the decision. I guard my heart and watch my thoughts. I don't need one more book, as it comes and goes from my mind's eye. If I am to read this book, it will come again to my awareness in an explicit invitation.

Example 2: About Wearing the Habit

To make a decision is difficult for individuals but even trickier for groups. This example below is about a group wrestling with choices that at first seem simple. We could have said that each monk or nun could decide for himself or herself, but we chose to use this opportunity to learn discernment and decision making through prayer and intentional discrimination.

In 2009 I was teaching sustained *lectio divina* to novices at Roscrae, a Cistercian monastery in Ireland, and we had the occasion to dialogue about wearing the habit. During the week, we took an excursion to Clonmacnoise, the monastic ruins of St. Kieran. The group of nineteen was made up of monks and nuns from England, Scotland, Wales, and Ireland. The Clonmacnoise settlement goes back to the late 500s when St. Kieran (Ciaran) founded a monastery in a well-traveled route connecting the mid-section of Ireland from west to east.

After the official tour, we fit ourselves into the roofless chapel of St. Kieran and said one of the little hours of the Divine Office, None: a hymn, psalms, Scripture reading, petitions, Our Father, and hymn to Mary. The blessing and dismissal rite were profound. Bowing, I saw all our feet planted in that sacred womb in the midst of ancient tombs.

While words never express or contain the magnitude of experience, it is important to mark this occasion: junior Cistercian monks and nuns poised to make solemn vows to give all of their life, the whole of their life, to God under an abbot and a rule, following the monastic way of life.

Prior to this excursion, we had to decide not if we would go but what would be our attire. This second example of discernment is about the step-by-step process that we used to come to the decision to wear our monastic habits on this holy pilgrimage. We used the question of whether they wear their monastic habit or street clothes on this excursion to learn a discernment method to make decisions as a monk or a nun. My next lecture when we returned from the outing was a reviewing of a method of discernment.

Following is a summary of our discernment process.

Topic: The habit. The question: What does God want? Do we wear the habit or not? How do we know God's will? Which way? Which thoughts are sourced in God?

We used a method of sorting out thoughts to see what is the will of God. We watched our thoughts (this differs from thinking as it observes the thoughts rising):

From self: What would people think? The white habit worn by the Cistercian monastics might get soiled. It might rain. It would be nice to relax and get out of the monastic ethos for a while. It has been an intense week.

From evil: If we wear the habit, we can get admission without payment. It's good for management to lose profit. They owe it to us because we've taken the vow of poverty and others have to take care of us. The habit is a good cover for us to make others respect us. We deserve special treatment even if they need to suffer a little on our behalf.

From God: We can bear witness; we can be in tune with all the monastic saints who have gone before us. We can be in solidarity with each other in our resolve to make vows. We can pray as a group. We can become who we are trying to be.

From others: We need to give witness to the fact that our monastic life isn't just a job with a uniform.

The class virtually lived into wearing the habit the rest of the day. The next morning, we went around the room and asked each what they heard in their discernment.

We also asked if they heard a confirming sign that the resolve was the will of God. We talked about what would constitute a confirming sign. Some of the confirming signs were small: hearing the birds sing loudly indicated that it would not rain. There were some that had no clothes other than their monastic robes. The authenticity of going to the monastic ruins invited the monks and nuns in the program of formation to become more of what they were: monks and nuns. It was not just a site visit but an encounter with their own quest of joining the monastic way of life.

The individual polling was eighteen for and one against wearing the habit. The one against had profound reasons, but he easily switched to the group, as he wanted to be of one heart and one mind. The decision was made: to wear the habit.

After we came back that day, we reviewed the decision-making process and the benefit of the felt experience. All felt happy that we followed God's way. The experience we had was of harmony, single-mindedness, decorum, and deep joy. The travel was easy and without incident. It rained as we boarded the bus and when we got back on the bus, but during the couple of hours that we visited the site, there was no rain, only a mild breeze as we walked the tidy spring green walkways.

Nineteen monks and nuns walked where thousands have gone before! The junior monks and nuns decided to wear their habits to the shrine. After we returned from the Clonmacnoise ruins, we took a deeper look at monastic identity. To know who we are, we put on what we want to become. Then, we progress into the "real" that once was "ideal." The habit is a portable cell that protects and instructs us. To have identity, we need that solid knowing from deep inside. Identity requires entity, which is that firm boundary that specifies limitations to protect the choice of the identity. Tradition becomes our teacher. To have identity, we draw a circle to protect what is in the circle and identify what is outside its realm. The decision to wear the habit left no option to come to the excursion as a casual tourist.

The decision made as a group was done through prayerful discernment. They decided to go to the hallowed site wearing the habit of professed monks and nuns. Decisions become discernment when the Holy Spirit is heard and heeded.

Example 3: What Do I Do in My Cell?

This method of making a discerned decision is without steps. This is entering into a teaching of a revered elder that can be accessed through his or her writings. What is different about this method is that I had already decided to enter into my cell but did not know how to live in it as a nun. This is implementing a decision. Often we make the right decision but don't change: we keep up our former way of life in a new setting. No conversion happens.

I did this meditation that was in the form of a dialogue with this holy elder. I wanted to restart my interior life in a new cell (year fifty in my monastic life!). I recently moved into a smaller cell. I sorted out my things and brought into this space that which fostered my monastic way of life and distributed all else to be used by others. I even got permission to give away my 1957 alto saxophone to my first cousin, Dick Funk, who will hand it on to his grandson, Axl Funk.

Now, in the cell I had an opportunity to resume living the way I did in my former cell, except with fewer things. But the decision here was to go deeper into training of the mind, wrestling with my afflictions, doing sustained *lectio divina*, and doing whatever it took to prepare and rest up from the observances.

I first asked if this was the right question needing deliberation. Was this cell my new work, my inner work for these years? My virtual decision was to study and incorporate as much of Nil Sorsky's teachings[1] as would be appropriate for me in Beech Grove, Indiana.

After several weeks of *lectio*, I wrote the following imaginary dialogue:

Meg: Thank you for agreeing to an interview, Abba Nil. I just moved into a smaller cell and want to restart my practice of solitude, silence, and stillness. May I ask you a few questions?

Abba Nil: Certainly, but remember I lived in fifteenth-century Russia, which is vastly different from twenty-first-century Indiana.

Meg: Yes, but we have to start someplace. The desert spirituality of St. Benedict's sources in his Rule gives me hope. I have found your teachings refreshing, and with your help and the grace of God maybe we can bring them forward into our situation.

Abba Nil: It is similar, insofar as monastic life in my day was split like it is in your time. Your split is between apostolic ministry and contemplative monastic life. The apostolic sisters see their vocation as healing, teaching, witnessing, and serving "out there" on mission. You prefer that the monastic way of life—the original monastic impulse—be the mission. In my day, there was a split between small simple hermitages, or *sketes*, and the large land-owning estates that monasteries amassed. It's the same split between preference for the inner life and preference for the outer life. There is danger for the ministry when those in outreach are mindless of their own afflictions. The risk with those of us who prefer solitude is that we can get hostile toward others and become self-centered instead of follow the cross of Jesus into self-sacrifice. In truth, all of us do both: take the inner journey of asceticism and the outer journey of selfless sacrifice.

Meg: I have no desire to take on the macro-structures. The secular priesthood of the Roman Rite and the missionary societies of religious communities have an amazing history of apostolic accomplishments through outreach of social services. I'm a member of Benedictine sisters in America who favor the mission model. But now that I've been a Benedictine nun for fifty years, I'd like to at least dedicate my cell to solitude, silence, and stillness. Can you help me?

Abba Nil: Certainly. You've done your homework from the tradition. I did my homework before I became a hermit. I traveled to Constantinople, Palestine, and Greece. What was life-changing for me was the time I lived at the monastery of Mount Athos. I was smitten by *hesychasm*. When I returned to my home monastery, Kirillo, I found no openness to more of an eremitic way of life, so I decided to leave and pursue this plan: By the Sora River, in an isolated and swampy area, I founded a hermitage. This was a *skete*, based on the desert hermits and the practice of Mount Athos.

The *skete* is a hermitage for no more than two or three hermits, an elder and younger disciple(s). We pursued a schedule and routine of practice of our own devising, usually engaging in continuous prayer, reading, writing, and the editing and copying of manuscripts and crafting of icons and religious articles to be exchanged for provisions. Our time and energies were entirely individual and suited for solitaries. What we had in common was the store of food from donations and the availability of the elder for counsel. As hermits, we were not to engage in moneymaking labor, and though we gardened or foraged for ourselves, copying manuscripts or writing icons produced alms. Our work was as artisans. When we had enough, we gave to the poor instead of maintaining storage. Another work we did was to help those who came to us. The work was discernment. We helped everyone who came to know and practice God's way for them.

Meg: A hermitage or a *skete* is not possible for me in my lifetime. Is there a way I can have a taste of it in my cell?

Abba Nil: Yes, of course. Perhaps I should describe what we were doing and why, and then we can discuss how you could do some form if it in your situation. First, we attended to our environment. We made sure that our motives were to seek God and not to withdraw from work, civil engagement, or personal responsibilities. We felt that we could not hold our own in the environment of Russia during our times. We needed to go apart to attend to the inner life. You call it solitude or the observance that protects silence and stillness. We prepared for the struggle of the inner thoughts by first reducing the attachment to outer relationships, conflicts, attractions, and irritations. We had no models to guide us and there were few teachers who knew the tradition and could instruct us. We had to go to the teachings themselves, those holy writings that described a Christian form of living the spiritual life that had its roots in the first hermits who fled into the barren deserts of Egypt and Syria during the fourth century.

The *hesychasm* we inherited was based on the core school of Sinai, which included Nilus of Sinai, John Climacus, Hesychius of Sinai, Philotheus, and Pseudo-Macarius. This school of thought was advanced in the eleventh century by Symeon the New

Theologian. The revived *hesychasm* of Gregory of Sinai in the fourteenth century took root in Mount Athos, where I resided for a while and experienced it firsthand. And, of course, like your Father Benedict, I read the early desert fathers. From Evagrius I retrieved the sense of intellectual contemplation and his insistence on the central role of asceticism with the notion of withdrawal, disengagement, and nondesire in *apatheia*. From Pseudo-Macarius comes the trajectory of solitude and silence culminating in *penthos*, the sense of smallness of self, compunction, humility, and the gift of tears.

Meg: So you did not invent the *skete* model, but you studied the teachings and also tasted an expression of it when you were at Mount Athos?

Abba Nil: Yes, when I established our Sora hermitage, I had immersed myself in the literary sources of the desert tradition, and I also had experienced the practices of *hesychasm* by doing them myself. Of the two things, study and practice, it is more important to practice. Wisdom springs up from inside simply by reading the gospels and celebrating the Holy Mysteries and doing one's practice.

Meg: So you brought forward *hesychasm* to Russia in the fifteenth century. Again, my question is how can I do just a little part of it in my cell?

Abba Nil: Certainly, the cell is the place to start. Physical solitude is essential. I insisted that monks would take care of their bodies so they would be strong for the exertion of the inner work. The cell should be first of all a place of rest. Second, it should be away, that is, separate from others. This outer boundary provides structure for the individual person to bring the body, mind, and soul toward his or her desire for union with God. This outer boundary of solitude is joined with spatial practices of silence. There should be withdrawal from speech, hearing, seeing, and touching. Yet, we know that all the boundaries do not help if the mind is allowed free-fall thinking.

Meg: I know that dynamic well. I can be in my cell or in choir while my mind is rehearsing conversations with others that seem to be virtual, right there with me.

Abba Nil: John Climacus describes silence as an intellectual and mental process of withdrawal of concern and desire. This process purifies the mind and inner attention. It empties the mind of thoughts and provides for a still-pointedness or thoughtlessness, in the sense of possessing nothing, not even desiring to possess anything.

Meg: This is rigorous! It's worth it, though, to obtain purity of heart. Do you think it is possible in one lifetime?

Abba Nil: We have ways of doing this. You call them "tools." To maintain this purity of heart and mind, the church fathers and mothers recommend prayer, continuous prayer that fills the body, mind, and soul. This state of emptiness, maintained by continuous prayer, is called *hesychia*, meaning stillness, quiet, tranquility, and serenity. The function of continuous prayer, then, is to serve as a mechanism for maintaining vigilance and focus. In Greek, the term *nepsis* refers to vigilance or sobriety. Evagrius calls it *praxis*, the practice of virtue that purifies the passions or emotions. Other terms might be "prudence," "discretion," or "self-discipline."

Meg: We are back to the eight afflictive thoughts. Yes, there is no escape; those afflictions need to be rooted out. They are an obstacle to prayer that evolves into the ideal taste of tranquility and stillness. What tool do you recommend?

Abba Nil: We started with the practice of the Jesus Prayer. In your cell you can devote explicit practice toward ceaseless recitation. We taught physical techniques for breathing and posture. Very soon, when the afflictions subside, the thinking mind relaxes and the Jesus Prayer drops to the heart.

Meg: The Jesus Prayer. I've seen great benefit from this comprehensive way of prayer that is rooted in our Christian tradition.

Abba Nil: Yes, it is normal to experience from time to time "ineffable joy."

Meg: Can we return to the afflictions for clarification? Can the Jesus Prayer or the practice of remaining in solitude in our cell reduce the anxiety and fears of our emotions?

Abba Nil: Yes, of course. There is a certain amount of facing those fears and anxieties, but then quickly notice the triggers and first risings of these afflictive thoughts that become emotions. As you practice ceaseless prayer, you will notice that these afflictions do not come as frequently or with the same intensity and can be shifted out in a few hours or a few days. Before your cell practice, you might have carried these afflictions in the mind for months and years. Prayer has an anointing factor, soothing the emotions. The edges get rounded and the soft desire for God rises quickly and prevents that digging in of guts and grit that grasps our psyche.

Meg: So I enter my solitude and watch my thoughts? I do *lectio* and ceaseless prayer? Do I need to practice stillness physically, as in sitting in a meditation posture?

Abba Nil: There are two ways to enter into stillness. One is to still the mind; the other is to still the body. When we do both, there's great peace. Yet, I do *not* recommend yogic techniques. In your way of life they are too much too soon. You would do well to calm your mind and sit in your upright chair and breathe naturally, all the while doing your ceaseless prayer. Also, ordinary manual labor helps move stress out of the body. But, as you know, that work must be done with a mind at peace and always refrain from afflictive thoughts. The mind can be strong like the body with proper nourishment and balance of exercise and rest.

Meg: Emotional stillness is also part of the *hesychastic* tradition?

Abba Nil: Yes. Most of the brothers and strangers who sought us out were looking for ways of inner consolation and emotional steadiness. We had learned the art of listening and the ability to direct souls. We learned this not from others but from the teachings and our practice. And the practice is to deal with your thoughts!

Meg: Yes, thoughts matter!

Abba Nil: Once you have tasted that calm abiding silence, there is peace and tranquility. When you are steeped in and deep into this level of ceaseless prayer, agitation and noise are no bother. They are not heard. This is deep peace and the book of nature spreads out further and further to the delight of the senses.

Meg: But we never get beyond the eight afflictive thoughts, do we?

Abba Nil: We must never let down our guard, as the Evil One is even more subtle and seductive.

Meg: I'd appreciate a short form of your teachings on the thoughts.

Abba Nil: Gluttony is overcome by recalling the fleeting-
ness of consuming and the corruption of food. Eat
sufficiently but always short of fullness. Stop so as
to be a little hungry still. Eat whatever is placed
before you.

Fornication is overcome by confession and by
avoiding excessive self-recrimination. Avoid all contact or conversation that stimulates temptation.

Covetousness includes not just gold and silver
but clothing, tableware, tools for manual labor—
any material object. For necessities, obtain only
what is "cheap, unadorned, and easily obtainable."[2]
Conquering covetousness means not merely doing
without but not even desiring.

Anger is the recollection of things done and the
desire to avenge them. Cut off memory and thought.

Sadness is a form of self-pity and leads to despair, impatience, and sloth. In sadness one perceives oneself as disposed and abandoned to griev-
ous hardship by God. Don't "exaggerate with our
human ideas these hardships."[3] One must stop
complaining and disengage from imagined persecution. Mourn our weakness in order to foster
repentance, not out of sadness.

Acedia follows sadness and is a bane to those
"who live the solitary, silent life,"[4] because of the
necessity of meeting burdens unsupported and
alone—another positive argument for the *skete*.
While it may be good to persist alone in one's cell,

it may be better to converse with "someone skilled and edifying in the spiritual life."[5]

Vanity is the assumption of worthiness and praise of corrupt actions. Vanity is the precursor of pride.

Pride is a form of spiritual uncleanness, an arrogance extending externally the weakness of vanity. Pride's sources are many: material success, conduct, intellect, family, class, and talent. Human achievements easily engender pride. Recalling the sum lowliness of our situations as human beings, our dependence, and our transient natures thwarts pride. Nonassertiveness, acceptance, and the extirpating of desire combat the causes of pride.

Meg: These are timeless, and I have had bouts with each of these afflictive thoughts.

Abba Nil: If we keep mindful of our death and view this life as fleeting, we will refrain from being caught up in the temptations of the thoughts.

Meg: The best part of your teachings is to say that we will have, now, silence without anxiety.

Abba Nil: The cell is a place to release attachments. We can't even be attached to our cell!

Meg: The wisdom here is so attractive. And from your teachings I can see and understand the ascetical practice of "no anxiety." Stillness is the observance rather than simply a grace given to the virtuous.

Abba Nil: Yes, peace, stillness, long periods of no anxiety is the path. The inner journey is difficult at first, but sweet, mostly sweet.

Meg: Could you give me a blessing? I'll be on my way now. Thank you for this interview.

Abba Nil: Peace be with you.

Now I will guard my heart and watch my thoughts for ones that could challenge the decision of reclaiming solitude, silence, and stillness in my cell. It's a firm direction, on my part, to make my cell practice a lifelong habit, God willing.

Essentials of Discernment to Make Decisions

We have seen three examples of making decisions using methods of discernment: about reading a book, about wearing the habit, and about practice of the cell. What is essential to each of these decisions is to bring the question to prayer, ask with the attitude of indifference, and wait for the answer to come from God. We can learn from reading, from sorting our thoughts as we live into the question virtually, or we can do a sustained dialogue with a teacher, such as Abba Nil Sorsky. This dialogue could have been with St. Benedict, using quotes from the Rule, or with our Lord using the gospel texts, or it could have been with John Cassian. But the point is to listen as a disciple and be subservient to a wise elder.

A confirming sign is a typical way the Holy Spirit communicates to those of us seeking to do God's will but having difficulty making those choices for right action.

Teaching on Confirming Signs

In the Hebrew Bible the law is an instruction. Abiding with the directives of the law was the revelation to the people of Israel.

> Surely, this commandment that I am commanding you today is not too hard for you, nor is it too far away. It is not in heaven, that you should say, "Who will go up to heaven for us, and get it for us so that we may hear it and observe it?" Neither is it beyond the sea, that you should say, "Who will cross to the other side of the sea for us, and get it for us so that we may hear it and observe it?" No, the word is very near to you; it is in your mouth and in your heart for you to observe. (Deut 30:11-14)

Compliance with the law is a living dialogue with an inner invitation to remain in this abiding relationship with God as expressed in the gospels. This use of the law was about sorting thoughts and relying on one's ability to see sources and directives as a way of life. The confirming sign is merely a corrective to missing the obvious. We often miss the obvious because of our tendencies toward selfishness or habitual accommodation of what worked before must be the way to go now. So, once again, what are the criteria of a confirming sign?

We inform our conscience through study and knowing the law and moral instructions, but to know from the inside, as to what to do, we ask the Holy Spirit. We can trust this voice once we've learned how to separate out the voices—from self, from evil, from others, and from God. In the New Testament, the law was revealed in the person of Jesus Christ. We conform to this sign and live the way he did and taught. Instead of a dialogue with Nil Sorsky, I could dialogue with Jesus through one of the gospel stories. But since we have the example above of a dialogue with Abbot Nil Sorsky, I will continue teaching discernment through this example: How do I know God's way for me in my cell? What are the confirming signs pointing to here?

First, the sign must pertain to the question at hand. What made me move into a smaller cell? What gave me the permission to ask Abba Nil Sorsky, "What's the purpose and function of a cell?" What was it in the abba's writings that made me trust that he would have something to say that would pertain to me, living in an urban monastery in Indiana five hundred years after he lived in a rural setting in Russia?

The reason I trusted Nil Sorsky's teachings was because he taught his monks how to live the monastic life through the discipline of a cell. This question for me was timely because this was my fiftieth year as a nun and I had an opportunity to shift into a new cell. It was a time in which I could take a step to sort my things, to retool my arrangements, to order the few things that I do in a cell: sleep, maintain health and decorum, do *lectio*, write, rest, enjoy silence, immerse myself in edifying art, and maintain writing tools. Yet, if my monastic way of life was not just a lifestyle, all external forms needed to be arranged for that purpose. I had renounced a lifestyle of comfort and self-growth. I was ready to work in a steady fashion to be more mindful of, conscious of, alert to, and at the service of this vocation of seeking God. Many of my things were good things but pertained to my former way of life as a superior or facilitator of group process or student of this or that certification. Some were little things from travels or gifts from friends. The confirming sign was to contract, not to expand: what helped me be a nun today? I also wanted to make sure I was not keeping things that others could use. The gospel directive to be always mindful of the poor keeps me from maintaining an inventory of things I do not need when others could benefit from them now.

Second, there's a sign that not only pertains to the question at hand but also comes from the outside. I know I did not invent or bring it on myself. I could trust that this meditation with Nil Sorsky was a teaching from someone who had gone before me and could give me sound advice about how he did it in his time and how I can do it in my time. I actually studied the whole of his writings as they've come down to us in English. In the total context of his life, I saw his holiness, his wisdom, and his strong directives for me to shift my bedroom to a cell. A bedroom is in service of me, of my health, and of my well-being. A bedroom is in service of the self. But a cell is a teaching tool for my spiritual life. A cell teaches me selfless service and sacrifice. A cell is preparation for death. I realized that I would never have the chance to be a hermit, nor would I ever work under a monastic master teacher, but I do have their teachings.

A third criterion for a confirming sign is how it sheds light and prompts the joyful grace to get about doing the shift. The sorting of my cell was no longer just an aspiration but a realistic option for implementation. I did it and did it swiftly in a couple of days. The sorting was not painful, nor was it a sluggish resistance to muscular grit to do the right thing with force and fierce effort. It was natural, timely, and full of positive outcomes. Everything fit, and nothing was missed; all choices were easy and came with a low intensity of energy and with calm mindful work. My only ambivalence was about my alto saxophone: did I need it anymore? I seldom played it. I had three little recorders for playing with Sister Harriet, as I still took music lessons on Monday afternoons. What I did was take the sax to the music room for six months while I did a separate discernment process before I gave it away with permission. But I moved it out of my cell. My criterion for selecting things to go into my new cell was that each thing had to contribute to my monastic way of life. If it did, then I made room for it. If it did not, I sorted it out. Things in my cell became a means of grace for me as I discerned what contributed to my monastic way of life. What did I need to live it? As I said earlier I no longer needed my 1957 alto saxophone. The instrument has done its work. My cousin and his grandson will enjoy it. Notice that renunciation is accompanied by right feelings. I'm not giving up the sax, but handing it over with satisfaction and joy. I now play my descant, tenor, and base recorders with Sister Harriet.

If I apply those three criteria to my decision about reading or not reading the book by Karen Armstrong, there's a similar pattern, and in the end the confirming signs confirmed the decision not to read the book.

First, the book was there for my taking, but I was not at that retreat house to do another study on interfaith dialogue. I was to give a retreat and be there for the sisters who came for the retreat. To say no to this major book was saying no to a major study that would have taken me into my own little world that pertained to my former way of life.

The directive had less to do with taking me away from the focus of the retreat, however, than it had to do with my own stage on the contemplative journey. I am on the other end of reading thousands of books on this and that. Between 2003 and 2004, when I had some troubles with my eyesight, I refrained from reading. This was a wonderful opportunity to go silent, deeper into the realm where thoughts rise slowly in one-at-a-time fragments. Insights discover layers and layers of substance at work, knitting together opposites and the category of the new. In a sense, the work took on its own life. Then, when I was able to read again, the words were richer and more meaningful than before. Again, I always had the insight that I was not inclined to know more but to be more knowing. The decision not to read the hefty, comprehensive volume of Karen Armstrong was to set my boundaries. I knew enough and did not have the directive from the Holy Spirit to know more.

Second, the confirming sign came from a direction outside of my usual patterns. I always picked up a book and read it at the place and left it behind. It was a kind of hobby to make a find and enjoy a gift of the place, the trip, or the conversation with someone in my travels. It was rather a blow to my ego that I had no business taking on that book while I was assigned there to do something else. It was an outside force that said, "Take that book back to the library. Not now and not for me." The subtle part of this directive was to know that my tendency was to study, study, study and become more immersed into a topic, an author, or another way of teaching a subject. This habitual student characteristic had served me well up until about ten years ago.

Since then, there has been a shift from the head to the heart. Less is more. At this stage of my life I prefer hours and hours of silence and not more inner chatter in my mind. Ceaseless reading was getting in the way of my ceaseless prayer. I was overthinking. Some of this reading caused me to be confused, disturbed, and insatiable about one more way of speculation about God. I was not getting enough rest at night. To function, I'd require a nap during the day. Now I heard from the Holy Spirit that my reading requires me to be selective and guided by the Holy Spirit.

The third confirming sign was the joy, the relief, and the humor to take back that big book just one day after I signed it out. That book pertained to my former way of life when I was doing monastic interreligious dialogue. Now, I was giving a retreat on *lectio divina*. It wasn't for me. I was being seduced by a book and might have missed wonderful walks in the woods around the lake in the autumn of beautiful southern Indiana. The book was about God, but without the book I was "in" God. It's always easier to do the right thing!

Decision Making without Steps

Since we make decisions all day long and with a habit of doing our best, we might not feel inclined to step back and work through the five steps systematically. To approach a decision as a story might be helpful to us from time to time.

A choice comes to my attention. I can do this or not do this action. What makes a decision "discernment" is asking the Holy Spirit to come and guide me. I then approach the moment like a story that unfolds in my mind before I actually decide and do it in real time.

The moment is now, and the choice is mine, but I explicitly ask the Holy Spirit to help me. Then, I pause. This prevents compulsive reactions that I might regret or sometimes have to undo with many more decisions that could have been prevented. The pause is a moment to review the story in front of me. In the story, I see in my mind's eye the past, present, and future gathered together in one place.

This sounds odd, but we all have this experience. We step back, and there's a moment here that is bigger than the actual time on the clock. This moment stores the impulse of grace. In the story, I see how I can direct my actions. I know. But I remain in pause mode for an instant to hear the little confirming sign, that impulse of grace.

Then, I act.

Sometimes I am still mistaken, but God knows my heart, and I really do want to live a discerned life and listen with the ear of my heart. The early elders taught that one could rely on the rule and obedience to one's superior. This teaching is profound, but since sometimes superiors have not done their inner work on their afflictions, there's huge risk in taking their word literally. Our inner work is so sacred that we cannot rely on anyone else. But the teachings on obedience are helpful. Here is a short summary.

Obedience for Beginners

Early sources of the desert elders require newcomers to fall into the daily rounds of work and prayer. The *horarium* (schedule of the day) is an important immersion into the culture. Benedict takes only two chapters to talk about obedience, but he uses fourteen chapters to lay out the schedule of the day, the seasons, and the *ordo* for arranging what goes on at the time of prayer. This preference for behavior conformity is the training. To be a nun, clothes are even ritually bestowed. Since the Second Vatican Council, we no longer wear the traditional habit that was worn and only slightly modified in the last fifteen hundred years. A new fashion will emerge that fits our way of life. In the meantime, most of us wear simple, understated, functional clothes. We follow the rigors of daily prayer, meals, study, and work.

The roles of leadership and services are prescribed for the sake of institutional life but are vehicles of training in obedience. The theory behind these observances was that, by conforming to "the way it is done," one can then bring into alignment one's thoughts and dispositions toward prayer and an abiding inner relationship with God. When these observances are a habit and when one's mind is in tune with one's regular actions through this obedience to others, one gradually learns to trust one's inner obedience while doing what the group does. This obedience is conforming to the directives of the Holy Spirit.

Obedience is an observance that others can see. The preference is quality but not mechanical formality. Obedience is a culture that carries the intent of the group. A visitor can see for herself the good zeal of the individual or the group being on time, walking, standing, and sitting with decorum. A novice can trust that keeping the *horarium* "keeps her." Obedience is not only a directive by the leader (abbot or prioress) but also a directive by the group (mutual obedience). Observance is the first degree of commitment. The second degree is practice, those ways within the observances that monastics conform to the guidance of the Holy Spirit. The major practices are silence, prayer, work, hospitality, common meals, common study, and common meetings. And within the practices is *praxis*. This inner work, called *praxis*, is done in the mind while conforming to the practices that round out the observances. So, while in prayer or at common table or doing one's manual labor, the mind continues ceaseless prayer and recollection (as described in chap. 2).

The gift and benefits of obedience move us toward the gospel incarnated in our midst. We feel the peace of all energies focused and moving us toward our heart's desire. We participate in groups that promote the gospel values in our midst. We experience peace through the direction of the Holy Spirit's guidance. Listening to this inner voice directs our interior work. We prepare for the teachings that pertain to practice and *praxis*.

Obedience, following directives from another, is the first step of discernment. If we are already doing the right thing that has been handed down through custom of thousands of years of the monastic way of life, then we are ripe to hear that soft, gentle voice of the Holy Spirit. Our personal choices, personal degrees of practice, respond to the gentle invitations of a closer relationship with the Lord that is found in the mind's eye or the inner and vast secret realms of the heart.

It seems that while obedience is first-level conformity and training for mystical voices to rise, there's no breaking point where I can cast off obedience and say that I'm above it or don't need it any more. There's much conversation that being a hermit (eremitical tradition) is a higher vocation than is living in community (cenobitic tradition). Most monasteries require obedience from their hermits. They are still tethered to the community and the abbot.

Christianity requires us to be at the table of the Eucharist and in service of one another. Obedience has a public and outside dimension that is never fully cast off in this lifetime because of our inherent tendency toward ignorance and self-delusion. A particular problem today is cunning. This affliction is a form of pride that the novice employs to trick the director into the mistaken notion that the novice is prematurely enlightened. Both fall, and it harms the group who then dismisses inner work as unnecessary for the monastic way of life. Discernment matters.

Spiritual direction can take many forms to help us make decisions and to root out our afflictions so that we can live life with a discerning heart. In the next chapter we will examine four options. We will also consider the delicate matter of a teacher, a director, a spirit-filled guide. In our times can we entrust our soul to another?

Chapter 4

Where and to Whom Can We Go for Discernment?

Biographies abound that report how a saint went off to the desert, to a cave, or to a prolonged retreat to hear the Word of the Lord. Today, there is frequently neither financing nor permission to leave assignments of work for an in-depth solitude experience. But it seems to be not an optional requirement if one is to go deeply into acquiring the Holy Spirit. This book prompted me to offer four options to retrieve this tradition of going apart to pray as our Lord did and as is reported in the gospels (Luke 4:1-2, 42).

What would a long retreat look like today? Given that we will need to stay at our home monastery as much as we can to learn the Rule and to maintain the critical mass of numbers of community at Divine Office, meals, and manual labor assignments, the extended retreat that is being proposed here is done mostly at home.

St. Enda[1] Retreat
(Ten, Thirty, or One Hundred Days)

One hundred days in St. Enda, which is symbolic for "in your own place," is a program designed for monastics who want to learn discernment from the early monastic tradition. This experience is up to the individual to start when ready by staying in the monastery where he or she has made vows. For maximum benefit, these one hundred days ought to be sequential. Only the third segment of thirty days needs to be in solitude away from one's usual routine. Exceptions are always possible, but the requirement of solitude and going deeper into stillness is the content of the last thirty days. If one remains "busy," the training effect remains diminished. Practice of discernment can only be learned by actual experience. The conceptual part will not be enough to initiate the monastic into this way of living from the heart. We begin with prayer to the Holy Spirit.

The first thirty days consist of practices that renounce our former way of life, the way we lived before we entered the monastery. We tend to take back our commitment in small ways, and, though we live in the monastery, we bring our worldly ways with us. To return to our first good zeal we do those little things that bring good order to our cell. We use our practices of decision making through the Holy Spirit by asking how to order our clothes, tools, and other things we use for music and the arts. We attend to our habits of eating and drinking. We check our balance of exercise, work, and study. During these thirty days the monastic is prompted to do whatever is necessary to take the next step to align relationships, health, accountability, usage of time, and patterns of service. The monastic reads the New Testament and memorizes three to five psalms. If the monk or nun has to work at his or her assignment, that is okay, but he or she takes on no extra commitments so that there is time for the work above. This St. Enda retreat is actual, not just a goal or an aspiration. It is to be observed with its practices and attention to *praxis*.

During the second thirty days, the monastic meets with an elder and remains in the monastery in his or her cell like usual, but the work is inner order rather than outer order. The monastic discerns, through prayer to the Holy Spirit, his or her particular affliction(s) and the tools to manage the same. The serious inner work begins. The revelatory text of one's sustained *lectio* is content for study. The monastic continues with another reading of the New Testament and memorizes two more psalms, along with the work on his or her revelatory text. To memorize St. Patrick's Morning Offering would be helpful for the next stage. The point is to have those verses in one's mind and heart to recall when on the thirty-day solitude retreat.

The final thirty days are spent residing in solitude either in one's own cell or, if possible, at a hermitage on the monastic grounds. The monastic sets up a check-in with the elder each day. The monastic elder sets up the program with the monastic, but the goal is maximum solitude, silence, and *praxis*. The monastic refrains from study and, instead of mental work, does an assignment of manual labor. A suitable cell for this time of *praxis* is essential. For this part of the program, the monastic's normal work and personal obligations need to be suspended for the sake of learning discernment through the Holy Spirit's guidance. Afflictions are rooted out and replaced by practices of prayer (tools).

Ideally, this would be on the Aran Island of Inishmore where one could follow the footsteps of St. Enda and his school for monks. The monastic would recite the memorized psalms walking to St. Brigid Church and to other holy sites on the island. It's best that this month be solo. The monastic sets this up and sustains the solitude on Aran Island or at another place where this inner work can be done. Group experiences create another dynamic and it is counterproductive to set up an alternative group, either virtually or actually. The training in discernment is to be done in one's vocation as lived in committed relationships.

The last ten days, the monastic returns home and goes back to work, but attention is given to *praxis* (thoughts while doing practices or observances). The monastic eases back into ordinary life, conforming to the monastic *horarium*. The completion of these one hundred days ought not be the completion of one's revelatory text, so ongoing sustained *lectio divina* continues. Afflictions are prevented from returning by a practice of ceaseless prayer. A ritual of conclusion is celebrated. This could be a mass of thanksgiving or a simple walk to the cemetery.

I have just finished doing this one-hundred-day re-treat myself while living in my home monastery. During winter months, the first thirty days of above-the-river agenda (code for "external life") got my attention, and I arranged my appointment and travel schedule so that I had the time, energy, and space to do all those little things that wait year after year for some lucky spurt of energy. I ordered my cell, clothes, music, archives, books, and things. I got my medical requirements from the deferred list to the done list. I made phone calls and completed a few writing projects that were pending. I restarted an exercise program and slept enough that fatigue lost its grip. I restarted getting to church and meals on time. I did extra duties around the monastery to be of service to those busier than I am. I found that I had plenty time for my sustained *lectio*—which was doing a continuous reading of the Bible.

The second thirty days, I listened to my afflictions. I saw that my speech was depreciative and needed stricter control from my heart. The tongue is so quick, and in our culture we talk so much! I craved more silence, but it was more to do with self-management than to pray and be a contemplative. I also observed that past afflictions with anger had diminished and no longer was my mind hooked on past hurts, worrisome cultural traps, or obsessive propensity to overwork.

The third thirty days were done right here in my cell. There was no way to get away someplace else. I had to learn solitude in my cell. The training in my cell was rigorous from the inside, and from the outside my whole retreat was invisible. While I had arranged a steady communication with a wise elder, I did not share. In not sharing and not being vigilant about ten of those days, I slipped back into ordinary time. Perhaps it is asking too much to stay in place, or could a stronger accountability arrangement with my wise elder have been enough to hold me to my resolve? Anyway, maybe next year during Lent I'll try to do these inner thirty days again, either in another place or with stricter accountability.

The last ten days is to return to a "new normal" discerning way of life. This part was wonderfully healing. I recommend this St. Enda retreat. I am sure it will be different for each monastic, but for me it was wonderful.

There are other ways to find the same place where God is dwelling in an abiding way. To serve others with wholeheartedness is both helpful to someone else and to the one who is transformed by doing the selfless service. Service won't purify the soul unless the ego steps aside and the Holy Spirit reigns.

Selfless Service

There is an alternative to the thirty-day solo retreat that would be as beneficial: selfless service that has the same discipline of preventing free-fall thinking. This might be called rigorous caregiving, such as doing night duty for the sick or an assignment that would require total abandonment of one's usual schedule and habits.

This also purifies the mind and implants the Gospel in the heart. As a prerequisite, this path also presumes good order of our monastic way of life and having a ceaseless prayer practice that keeps the mind steady and readies the heart for pure intentions. This active duty achieves the same fruits of the Spirit as does solo hermit time.

To train for this kind of work, one would need to have the skills of the cell practice: guarding the heart; watching thoughts; refraining from the afflictions of anger, dejection, vainglory, pride, or any other affliction that rises. Ceaseless prayer would have to prevail, as the person in need of care is suffering and the caregiver must be sustained in God's mercy to show compassion and have the wisdom to be helpful.

If this kind of care is one's usual work, then the whole one hundred days of St. Enda training would be helpful. The point here is that the thirty days of solitude and the thirty days of selfless service can do the same thing to purify the heart.

There are times when to leave home and go someplace else is the only way to jolt the mind into new ways of thinking and acting. The sacrifices inherent in travel provide the same benefit as suffering. We call this sacrament "pilgrimage."

Program of Pilgrimage

Pilgrimage is a tricky practice. We start with good zeal and then slide into entertainment, curiosity, shopping, and leisure. What makes a travel pilgrimage? To learn discernment and to shift from self talking to self, a travel to some destination has to be prompted by the Holy Spirit.

The destination ought to be a shrine of some recognition that venerates an encounter with God. It need not be famous or well documented, but the soil ought to emanate an energy that is felt. This energy that is stored on some sites quickens the soil. For most who visit Gethsemani in Kentucky, there's a felt holiness.

This travel ought to be more than a destination on the outside where an "I've been there before" conversation follows. This is a pilgrimage where we prepare as a pilgrim to receive the graces sought by going to that place. A pilgrim often walks, takes off shoes, fasts, or remains at the door to become empty and ready. Humility matters in pilgrimage. The preparation usually lasts several days or months longer than the travel and the staying in place.

The decision to go on pilgrimage can be made using the five-step discernment method. Sometimes the urge to travel is not to be honored. If it is to be pilgrimage and not just another trip, it ought to be from an invitation of the Holy Spirit.

The actual visit has peculiar properties, especially a receptivity to whatever happens there. No agenda is the best mind-set for "being there." The time is not spent but gently received. And, finally, the going home is essential. To be a pilgrim is only in service of one's residential commitment at the home monastery.

For monastics, we often get an invitation to visit another monastery. For it to be a pilgrimage in service of learning to listen with the ear of our heart, we need to discern if it is an invitation confirmed by the Holy Spirit. Then, we go and listen and receive graces to help us live our vows at home.

The option to be in spiritual direction with a wise elder is rare today, but monastics soon find out that there's more inner work to be done after the novitiate than there was during the years of formation. Here is a way to engage in that practice that I have found helpful.

Seasonal Visitation to an Elder

The four seasons are a universal round of beginning and ending cycles of life. We can check in with ourselves and be accountable to another on a regular basis using this natural rhythm. The early monastic tradition was to disclose thoughts to one's abbot or to an elder.

Perhaps in the flow of this book on discernment there is a fitting derivative that would be helpful. A monk or nun needs help for listening with the ear of the heart for big decisions such as taking a leave of absence or placing one's name up for elections or accepting a call to a certain role in the monastery or the local church.

There is an ongoing need for direction to confirm one's affliction, one's practice of prayer, and one's sustained *lectio divina*. Training in discernment would also be helpful during sickness or aging and preparation for death. The dialogue would be discerning the Holy Spirit's dwelling and detecting obstacles to grace. Often those obstacles are a thorny relationship, an affliction of depression, or the need to make a good confession to a priest.

What might be helpful is to have the ear of a wise elder for an ongoing conversation. The four seasons are good turning points to check in: fall, winter, spring, and summer correspond in the Northern Hemisphere to Ordinary Time, Advent, Lent and Easter, and Ascension and Pentecost. These liturgical seasons are purifying in and of themselves. In the Southern Hemisphere we know that the seasons are the opposite, but their progression continues in an orderly way. Even in the desert the seasons are apparent. The cycles are phases within phases, and each concentric circle has its moments. Here's a sample agenda for four visitations to an elder each year:

Fall Visit:
    Greeting! Prayer to the Holy Spirit
    Agenda: Rooting out dominant affliction
    Naming the affliction and its indicators
    Finding a tool to root it out
    Learning the five-step decision-making method
    Blessing and leave taking with promise to pray for
        each other

Winter Visit:
    Greeting! Prayer to the Holy Spirit
    Agenda: Reporting on dominant affliction

Reporting on the tool that you practice

Reporting on a decision that was discerned through the five-step method

Learning sustained *lectio divina* as a practice

Blessing and leave taking with promise to pray for each other

Spring Visit:

Greeting! Prayer to the Holy Spirit

Agenda: Reporting on dominant affliction and practice to root it out

Finding a tool to prevent the affliction from returning

Reporting on a decision made through discernment

Reporting on sustained *lectio divina*

Dialoguing about hearing and heeding the voice of the Holy Spirit

Blessing and leave taking with promise to pray for each other

Summer Visit:

Greeting! Prayer to the Holy Spirit

Agenda: Reporting on affliction, tools of practice, sustained *lectio divina*

Reviewing the outcomes of the decisions made according to discernment

Naming the mystical voice heard by the spiritual senses

Blessing and leave taking with promise to pray for each other

Notice what is not part of the conversations at these visitations: there's no soul searching and storytelling of one's journey. It starts with the present moment. If in the operative affliction there's a context, the story is told and reverently received. Then, the elder teaches a practice for the monastic to respond to these inner thoughts.

Notice that there's no review of literature, workshops, lectures, or conversations that are hashed through. One's relationship in faith to God, not speculative reasoning, is the content.

Notice that there is not the chain of friendship making. It's an elder with a role and a seeker who is learning to listen. These boundaries are worth keeping so that God is the center of the soul and these teachings have a solid home to do their work. This is sacred ground.

Notice that there's a deep conversation about the interior life. Questions of physical, psychological, and monastic drama are handled in other forums. The elder is in the desert tradition to tend to the soul who has gone apart to seek God.

This conversation does not replace other conversations that are necessary in a monastery for good order, healthy relationships, and well-being, but this visitation with an elder is about the spiritual journey.

The four seasons provide a sturdy framework, sequence, and support system for the monastic who wants to listen with the ear of her heart. But to do this we need to have confidence that we are meeting with a wise elder. What does the tradition say about finding an elder?

Pneumatikos *or Spiritual Father or Mother (Elder)*

Though this tradition of manifesting our thoughts is not often observed in our time, we can learn a great deal from it. How, for instance, do we recognize a wise elder? Would we recognize one if we saw one?

A wise elder is one who has tamed his or her thoughts and has compassion (meekness). This elder needs to embody the spiritual teachings in order to mediate to others the meaning of life. The tradition would say that one of the main criterion for a wise elder is to have the practice of ceaseless prayer, such as the Jesus Prayer. It would be self-acting and a continuous habit of prayer. This prayer practice would foster an infusion into the Holy Spirit, hence the nomenclature, *Pneumatikos*. This acquisition of the Holy Spirit might be so hidden that no one from the outside would know this about the elder.

If I, as a monastic, examine my conscience daily and lay my thoughts out weekly to a wise elder, which thoughts do I lay out? Most of the time I would give priority to my afflicted thoughts without analysis and then receive a short word from the elder. In response, I promise to pray for the elder and show signs of respect.

Notice the roles here: the monastic practices humility; the elder gives a discerned word. A teaching is given if the elder intuits that the monk or nun is ready and willing to do the word.

If there is no wise elder available, the monastic matches inner thoughts to teachings from the tradition as they are written in a rule or in Scripture. The role of the community is to embody the teachings of the tradition so those teachings thrive in a culture of acceptance and the monastery is a living embodiment of the tradition.

A wise elder also discerns where the thoughts are coming from: self, God, others, or evil forces. The elder can also listen not only for the words but also for the motivations, the intentions, and the subtle thoughts that may escape the thinker. The most helpful kind of elder teaches by example as well as by words from the tradition.

The monastic manifests the same thoughts over and over again as long as it takes to dismantle the affliction. The elder listens to the same material over and over again as long as it takes to deactivate the afflicted thoughts, feelings, or passions.

The goal is that the monastic will notice the first inkling of a thought or emotion before it becomes a full-blown passion. To notice this moment of consent and to sharpen one's will to let it go earlier and earlier before it cycles into habitual patterns makes it easier do the loving thing. This teaching is important: if the afflictive thought is deactivated, it is easier to do the loving things, but the monastic can do the loving thing even with the afflictive thought, and that compassionate action also calms the mind and dismantles the habits of afflictive thinking.

The elder can teach the monastic moderation. The middle way is safest. Extremes usually point to ego involvement and some form of pride. Moderation is not mediocrity but surrender of the will to a higher good, God.

This relationship between the elder and the monastic is sacred. The trap of exchanging gifts should be avoided because it may lead to dependency on either side. This relationship is a spiritual gift in and of itself. An exchange of material gifts gives room for dependency and obligations.

The level of confidence in this relationship is strict and as unbreakable as the seal of confession. Like all inner connections of the soul, it should mean a relationship the monastic can count on for a lifetime.

This practice of manifestation of thoughts faded from monasteries around the seventh century. As the eight thoughts were translated into the seven capital sins, the practice of manifestation of thoughts became combined with confession. The individual confession started out as a healthy pastoral practice that replaced the public humiliations of sinners in cathedral churches but soon became a ritual that paid attention only to the sin and not the thought systems that caused the sin. Also, the administrative types were elected abbots and abbesses, and pastoral time was neglected in favor of governing vast estates and little towns outside the abbey walls. In feudal times, monastic superiors sometimes were appointees of ruling aristocracy. Today, we have economic woes, low numbers of membership, and large facilities beyond our capacity to manage. As we understand our tradition, however, we can reclaim our heritage; living the life from the heart will refound our old establishments.

The logic of manifesting my thoughts goes something like this: if I'm not attentive to my thoughts, then sin gets my attention. The practice that helps me root out sin is confession or the sacrament of penance or reconciliation. If I am attentive to my thoughts, however, it makes sense to manifest them to someone for help *before* they coalesce into full-blown sins.

The Sacrament of Confession or Manifestation of Thoughts?

There are three major differences between confessing sins and manifesting thoughts.

First, the nature of sin is a violation of conscience. I confess, "I did wrong." Manifesting thoughts is simply the naming of thoughts one after the other. They are rising thoughts, and if identified early, often, and willingly, these thoughts have very little power over my will. "I am not my thoughts."

A second difference is that, when we are manifesting thoughts, it is not recommended that we to return to the past. This practice is a tool to see my thoughts now and to lay them out so that they have no more power over me. St. Benedict says that we are to dash them on the rock that is Christ (RB Prol. 28). Confession is naming a past thought, word, or deed that was done and is now regretted.

A third difference is that confession as a sacrament officially is to be administered by an ordained priest. It has a history, a ritual, and a symbolic meaning that is shared by Catholic Christians. The sacrament is experienced in the context of the larger ecclesial community. There are always exceptions to this formal reception of the sacrament of reconciliation. I have often received the confession of sin. When giving spiritual direction to someone who confesses, I ask the person to go to a priest for formal absolution when they get the first opportunity. God hears our prayers.

Manifestation of thoughts is the ongoing work of a monastic. It's a monastic practice that is regularly done to get at the earliest level of thought and not the end-stage result of sin. The devotional confession seeks the grace of the sacrament—forgiveness of sin. Manifestation of thoughts does not emphasize forgiveness of the sin but rooting out the habit, the thought patterns that cause sin. Manifestation of thoughts prevents a sin consciousness and is an exercise in feeling God's abiding mercy. Manifesting thoughts has no juridical feel to it. We are more like a child lifting up our innermost thoughts.

The position of elder in some Eastern traditions was passed down in the nonelected role of a *staretz*, but in the West the practice of manifestation of thoughts was simply supplanted and/or forgotten.

Can we have confidence in this old tradition, *exagoreusis*, from the Christian East? Perhaps it is happening more than we know. St. Benedict recommended this tool. It follows from the teachings on the eight thoughts that there are tools to reduce these afflictions. If there were a wise elder in our midst, we would lay out our thoughts simply and humbly. We would also ask her for tools that would help us.

As we know, we are not our thoughts, but they can trick us. So we need to lay them out in the light. We watch them in the presence of a wise elder who can also watch us watching our thoughts. In our own solitude in our cell we do this practice of guarding our hearts, but it is good to root out afflictions with the humble practice of disclosure in the light, in the presence of another's light that is not obscured. Their very own light (presence) can heal.

Again, this is the earliest form of the sacrament of reconciliation.

To prevent the affliction from getting activated, we observe its earliest moment. Like cancer, it is better to prevent it, or at least catch it early, than wait until it is a full-blown disease. Notice once again that we refrain from thinking about the content of the thought but watch its stage of development.

Manifestation of Thoughts to a Wise Elder

The desert tradition includes the longstanding practice of laying out thoughts to a wise elder. This practice was the earliest form of spiritual direction. The elder would receive the manifestation of thoughts and then give the monk a word, usually from Scripture, intended to break the cycle of thoughts from cycling around and around in the mind.

There was an admonition in the tradition "never to keep silent one's own thoughts. . . . This confession is barely conceivable without tears, or if it is done with no trace of feeling, one can conclude, that it is worth very little."[2] The admonition could be full of hope. There are thousands of stories of virtuous men and women.

In an unscientific "frequency analysis" of this foundational literature I've found these random insights life-giving:

- We are not our thoughts.

- Thoughts matter.

- Sins don't matter: Repent.

- Mercy is justice.

- Humility is wisdom.

- Silence teaches.

- Afflictions can be totally rooted out.

- The middle way is fasting.

- Extremes meet.

- Love is kind.

- Sweet tears don't weep.

- Sit with saints.

- Memory is the cell.

- Worship only God.

- Work is prayer.

- Anger divides friends.

- The guest is God.

- Demons flee.

- The tongue tricks.

- Stillness stays.

- God is the judge.

- All are saved.

The following are practical steps for manifesting thoughts to a wise elder:

- Lay thoughts out without commentary to be heard in the light.

- Back out the affliction as early as possible.

- The usual thoughts are food, sex, things (of the body), anger, dejection (of the mind), *acedia*, vainglory, and pride (of the soul).

- Aim to keep vigilant so to be prepared for the entities to rise.

- Aim to manifest an affliction as often as it rises.

- Be not surprised if the affliction rises with more emotion earlier and faster, with subtler promptings.

- Refrain from inner dialogue with the afflictions rising, especially self-justification and rationalizations.

- Refrain from daydream-like fantasy of either memories or plans to do such an encounter in the future.

- Confess with compunction of heart.

This tradition of having a wise elder is almost lost but can be retrieved, especially by monastics. First, like all practices, the only way to learn it is by doing it, and doing it with real life experiences. What is reported to me that seems most helpful is to simply start with an elder, and if that person isn't the right one, then God sees the sincere heart and the right one will appear.

Second, the key is to resist analysis, commentary, and contextual drama. The point is to back out or unthink into the origin of the rising thought.

Third, the process is the content rather than just a method to get at the content. For example, the monk ought to be not angry but calm, living in an abiding peace. It isn't really helpful to review the story line of the anger over and over again. It serves only to retraumatize the seeker into deeper and deeper grooves of the affliction.

Fourth, the goal is repentance and *conversatio* of our way of life.

It seems to me that in our times we cannot afford to lose touch with this tradition. It will open the door of our salvation and peace of heart; then, the monastic way of life will be natural and life-giving for others.

Through retreats, selfless service, pilgrimage, and manifestation of thoughts, we can, with grace, overcome our afflictions. We also have saints who have gone before us to be examples. We can imitate them by using our lives today if we understand what they were doing when they lived. St. Benedict and St. Patrick provide for us a living tradition.

Chapter 5

Imitating Those Who Went before Us

St. Benedict

Pope Gregory the Great immortalizes St. Benedict in his book, *Life and Miracles of St. Benedict*.[1] Even though this is a specific literary genre of hagiography, we can learn much from this text. We see Benedict's radical discernment in each stage of his life: We note his discretion when a student in Rome, in residence with his beloved nurse, then as a solitary, as an abbot of his host community, and, finally, as an abbot of his choice community. The Rule he wrote is widely followed today because of its middle way of moderation.

As a Student in Rome

Born in Norcia, Italy, Benedict was sent to Rome for school by his distinguished parents. He was enrolled in the honorable classical liberal education (mathematics, grammar, rhetoric, astronomy, literature). Most likely, he was being trained to become an attorney or political leader. Trade and crafts would have had a different curriculum—not liberal arts (training in being).

Benedict noticed that his peers were abandoning themselves to vice and worldliness. Benedict feared that what he was leaning toward was eternal ruin. "He wanted to please God alone," in the words of St. Gregory. He discerned to turn his back on further studies, give up home and inheritance, and resolve to embrace the religious life. "He took this step, fully aware of his ignorance; yet he was truly wise, uneducated though he may have been."[2] Benedict abandoned his studies. He renounced his former way of life as a student, went to Affile (modern Enfide) in the Sabine Mountains, and stayed near the Church of St. Peter (thirty-five miles east of Rome). His life took another turn because of his keen discrimination. He was awake to the sorrow of his maid who accidentally broke a valuable dish. Benedict prayed, even to the point of tears, and mended the dish. For doing this miraculous deed, Benedict was given public praise beyond his stage of humility. He was at risk to the evil forces of vainglory, so he discerned that he'd prefer to suffer ill treatment from the world rather than enjoy its praises.

In Solitude

Then he was drawn to complete solitude, which he found in a narrow cave near Subiaco, situated thirty-five miles east of Rome and north of Anagni on the Teverone. He was clothed with a monastic habit by the monk Romanus. Benedict wanted to spend himself laboring for God and not to be honored by the applause of humans. For three years Benedict stayed in this cave, later called the Holy Grotto. Romanus lived under the rule of obedience and training of Abbot Deodatus. He brought Benedict bread by lowering it to him on a rope. Benedict battled temptations from self and from demons. We hear the report from St. Gregory that Benedict experienced the challenges and same temptations that Abba Anthony encountered. The temptations of the flesh are said to have been so strong that Benedict rolled naked in thorns in order to be rid of them.

A story is recorded about the conclusion of his three years tended by Romanus. During Easter of Benedict's third year as a hermit, a priest came to break his fast. After several trials, both internal and external, Benedict had passed the discerning period of solitude and trained into living a life toward God rather than self or evil. As a result, he obtained from God a perfect tranquility that showed the success of his ascetical efforts.

Then, Benedict's place of solitude was discovered by shepherds. They brought him food, and Benedict taught them about God. His reputation spread swiftly in the area, and soon the monks of Vicovaro asked him to be their abbot. He left Subiaco to go the twenty miles to Vicovaro. We don't know how long Benedict stayed with these so-called monks, but they would not submit to his rule and obedience. The Vicovaro monks even tried to poison Benedict. Gregory quotes Benedict as saying, "Did I not tell you at the outset that my way of life would never harmonize with yours? Go and find yourselves an abbot to your liking. It is impossible for me to stay here any longer."[3] Benedict left. He made the decision to leave monks who preferred self-rule.

We hear, as the story continues, that Benedict "went back to the wilderness he loved, to live alone with himself in the presence of his heavenly Father."[4] So, we know that Benedict sorted himself out from the Roman students, from the adulating witnesses where he lived with his maid, from the training under Romanus, and now from the unfaithful monks of Vicovaro.

As Founding Abbot of Subiaco

Of the next moment of Benedict's discernment in chapter 3 of the *Life and Miracles of St. Benedict*, Gregory uses the famous dictum, "He came to himself!" It came to Benedict to be a founder of his own monastery. Benedict established twelve monasteries at Subiaco. Here, he had several smaller sets of monks, appointing a dean as his delegated authority over the monks in each monastery. St. Gregory reports that St. Benedict gained a reputation for miracles, conversions, and political influence for peace during very dark times in Italy, like Moses finding running water (Exod 17:1-7; Num 20:1-11), or like Eliseus with the iron blade that rose from the bottom of the lake (2 Kgs 6:4-7). The walking on the water recalls

St. Peter (Matt 14:28-29), the obedience of the raven is like Elias (1 Kgs 17:6), and the grief at the death of an enemy is like David (2 Sam 1:11-12; 18:33). Benedict was filled with the spirit of all the just. With allusion to stories of the prophets, St. Benedict is put in the tradition of a Pentecost immersion into the Holy Spirit.

At the original Subiaco monastery he encountered envy and jealousy of a priest from the vicinity who tried not only to slander and poison the saint but also to lead his disciples astray. Benedict made another major choice: to stop the corrosive dysfunction of the priest on his Subiaco system. He left again.

As Founding Abbot of Monte Cassino

Benedict revised his Subiaco system and founded Monte Cassino in 529. The entire community lived in one structure. This is the cenobitic model written about in the Rule.

As he was known for his discernment, Gregory the Great wrote, "Holy men do know the Lord's thoughts, Peter, in so far as they are one with Him."[5] Benedict interpreted God for his monks and those who came to seek spiritual direction from him.

The only one who bested Benedict was his twin sister Scholastica, who insisted Benedict stay in holy colloquy with her. What he would not do by grace, he was forced to do by nature when a storm kept him into the night in holy conversation with her. To depart from the edifying stories and commentary of St. Gregory written around

590, we know from our study of the Rule of Benedict that his discernment goes beyond himself and his saintly life. The Rule is a transmission of that great gift from the Holy Spirit mediated by Benedict to us. This Rule is our measuring cup, our ruler, and our compass for discernment.

We see in Benedict's life a student who renounced his former way of life; a hermit who preferred solitude to premature notoriety; and an abbot who renounced being led by wicked monks or being the object of a jealous, neighboring priest. With discernment and with the guidance of the Holy Spirit, he left all and founded a middle way for a community of monastics who seek God under an abbot and under a rule.[6]

We have different times but the same story—phases in our life to discern and take action, discern and take action. The method requires that we are awake and discern God's call over and over again. It seems that leaders need to discern carefully. Most of us ought not jump from being an academic student to being an abbot or a prioress without the school of solitude. There are times to quit school because there might be a more important degree for one's life's work. And, finally, being called by members to be a leader is a dangerous method of appointment unless we are in our own skin. Discernment continues over and over at each junction of our lives.

Benedict's Rule has as its genius an innovation that has served the monastic world for almost sixteen hundred years. This feature was his directive for moderation. He tempered the previous rules with doable but still discrete teachings on food, prayer, sleep, work, selecting an abbot, appointment of staff, clothes, facilities, visitors, artwork, liturgy, discipline, and the distribution of the psalms to be said at Divine Office. His Rule is brilliant in content; it is a redaction of earlier sources and a stitching together of a Western style of the monastic way of life. It is a masterpiece for training in discernment.

St. Patrick

Patrick wrote in his autobiographical *Confession*: "I am bound by the Spirit. . . . It is not just me, for the Lord Christ commanded me to come."[7] And in one of his letters Patrick wrote, "Was it without God or according to the flesh that I came to Ireland? Who drove me here— bound by the Spirit—to see no one who was related to me? (*Letter* No. 10)."[8] Again Patrick writes:

> Once again I saw him praying in me and I was as it were inside my body and I heard him praying over me, that is, over the inner man, and he was praying powerfully there, with groans. And during the whole of that time I was dumbfounded and astonished and I wondered who it was praying in me, but at the end of the prayer he spoke as if he was the Spirit, and so I woke up and recalled that the Apostle had said: "The Spirit helps us in our weakness; for we do not know how to pray as we ought, but the Spirit himself intercedes for us with sighs too deep for words."[9]

How did Patrick become such a mystic, an icon for many of us today?

Life and Confession

St. Patrick was more than a myth. He was a real historical character. He is known from only two short works, the *Confession*, a spiritual autobiography, and his *Letter to the Soldiers of Coroticus*, a denunciation of British mistreatment of Irish Christians. His life is dated somewhere between 389 and 493 CE; he lived to be in his seventies. He was born in Britain of a Romanized family and educated in a westernmost sector of Britain or Wales. His great-grandfather was Odissus, a deacon; his grandfather, Potitus, was a presbyter, or priest; his father, Calpornius, was a deacon as well as a decurion, or local magistrate responsible for the collection of taxes. At age sixteen he was captured by Irish raiders from the villa of his father and carried into slavery in Ireland. As a slave, he learned the local language of the Picts and Anglo-Saxons and endured much hardship. He was sustained by his faith in Christ. Six years later he awoke from a dream that advised him to travel two hundred miles toward Wicklow and board a ship to escape and go home. The travels were austere, and he and his shipmates almost starved to death, but once home he was on fire with the faith. He became a deacon and then was ordained a priest and eventually a bishop, appointed to return to Ireland to evangelize the furthest reaches of the known Western world. Though there were small bands of Christians present on the island, Patrick is credited for bringing the half-million population to Christianity. How did he do it?

Unlike other zealous evangelizers or warlords before him, St. Patrick, with unusual foresight, initially sought only the conversion of the kings, princes, and learned men, the Brehons, of Ireland. They were not only the leaders but also the ablest and most intellectual and therefore the more likely to grasp the significance of the new faith. There were no mass conversions or deadly wars that raided communities and imposed new regimes.

St. Patrick—a stranger and alone in a pagan, warrior-held land where the glory of physical prowess and combat, beauty and dress held pride of place—preached not in the lowliest cabins but in the great palaces. There, he braved the chance of the one word that would have sent him and his followers to their death. It was an epic adventure, and its lesson has never been forgotten.

It was the women who were first inspired by his wonderful story of the Mother and the Son and whose hearts pained with her sorrow at Jesus' sad and unmerited death. Women with children were the first converts. They were few enough, for St. Patrick's passage through Ireland was beset with trouble and trial at the beginning. Then the warmth of heart, the responsiveness, and the intellectual depth of the Irish Celts were drawn to the strange beauty of this new faith and its spiritual flame swept through the land.[10]

There are many myths and stories attributed to St. Patrick that are honored today by Catholics in the West. For the sake of this book on discernment, I want to raise up two aspects of his life that are particularly important for us and our times to learn discernment: First, he took his dreams seriously and acted on them, so much so that he became a missionary. Second, he used his suffering for training in faith and was filled with the good zeal of a Christ consciousness, like the apostle Paul. These two examples inspire us to do the same.

Dreams as a Way the Holy Spirit Comes

St. Patrick accepted his dream as inspiration from the Holy Spirit. He heard a voice that told him, "It is good that you fast, for soon you will return to your own country."[11] And another night it announced, "Come see, your ship is ready."[12] Patrick escaped and traveled from Killala Bay about two hundred miles from his master's house to a port in the vicinity of present-day Wicklow. He knew no one, but the ship of his dreams was there, ready to sail. Patrick was at first denied passage, even after he offered to work for it. Disappointed, he went away from the mariners and prayed. Before he had finished his prayer, one of the crew shouted after him, "Come quickly, for they are calling you." The shipmaster had been persuaded to take him aboard. Legend tells us the ship transported a supply of Irish wolfhounds bound to Nantes or Bordeaux.

Patrick sailed for three days with the heathen crew. The voyage was apparently uneventful. They landed near a desert or a land laid waste by war, and there was no fresh food to be had for twenty-eight days. Starvation threatened, and the shipmaster said to Patrick, "What do you say, Christian? You claim that your God is great and powerful. So why don't you pray for us? For we are in immediate danger of starving; we may not live to see another human being ever again." Patrick replied, "Trust with all your hearts in the Lord my God, for Him nothing is impossible, so that this day He may send you enough food for your journey until you are satisfied. For He has abundance everywhere."[13] Immediately, some wild pigs appeared on the road, and the starving men killed them, ate, and rested for two nights.

Already filled with the Lord, Patrick had another dream, a nightmare in which Satan visited him. He struggled and resisted the devil's temptation with the aid of Christ. There followed another nine days before the wayfarers met up with other men, and Patrick, guided again by a voice in his mind, stayed with his companions (now captors?) two more months.

They parted in Italy. Patrick found refuge in the monastic community of Honoratus on the Iles of Lerins, opposite of cape of Cannes. There is no evidence that he became a monk, but he at least had an experience of being hosted in a monastery that, by the fifth century, could have had over one hundred monks. He returned to his home in Britain and was ordained a priest.

Notice in his escape that there was a good dream from the Holy Spirit, upon which he acted, and it brought good fortune to him and others. He also had an experience of being visited by Satan in a nightmare. In this dream, he resisted the temptation and depended on Christ's help.

In another dream, he received his calling to return to Ireland. It is the best-known passage in the *Confession*. He tells of a dream in which one Victoricus delivered him a letter headed "The Voice of the Irish." As Patrick read it, he seemed to hear a certain company of Irish beseeching him to walk once more among them. "We ask you, holy boy, come back and walk among us once more." "Deeply moved," he says, "I could read no more." He also said of himself that he was "quite brokenhearted."[14] Yet he says that even on the night before he was to sail back to Ireland from Britain he was beset by doubts of his fitness for the task. Once he set foot on Irish sod, however, his hesitations vanished. Utterly confident in the Lord, he journeyed far and wide, baptizing and confirming with untiring zeal.

We have no way of knowing—based on his two writings that scholars deem to be historical—how Patrick was able to distinguish a dream from the Holy Spirit or a nightmare from the Evil One. But the fact that he records both kinds of sleep experiences is instructive. Not all dreams are from God and are invitations to follow the inspiration of grace. Some nighttime dreams are actually interventions of the Evil One that are simply temptations and are to be fought, with no action in one's deliberations. The crucial factor is to invite Christ to make known the source and follow only the visions that are from God. We know also that Patrick was known to go apart from time to time to listen to his heart.[15] Patrick found it necessary in the course of his conversion of Ireland to retire to the top of a 2,600-foot mountain, now known as Croagh Padraig, to replenish his spiritual resources. Be it in a dream or in solitude, discernment penetrates the heart, and the Holy Spirit manifests clear directives and energizes the soul.

Suffering

St. Patrick suffered, but with the grace of God he turned his suffering into a Christ consciousness. His suffering, both physical and emotional, was offered as prayer.

The story of St. Patrick is much like St. Paul's recounting of his tribulations on his four journeys and includes about every crisis one could encounter. Patrick was sold into slavery away from his homeland for six years, from age sixteen to twenty-three. He was a swine herder living outdoors in the harsh Irish climate of rain, wind, and frost, and he would have had to negotiate the wild boggy terrain. He learned a foreign language and was out of his Christian culture. His exile never seems abated. Even when ordained a priest, he was made a bishop with reluctance and was never honored during his lifetime, as he was not a man of letters and was rustic in style. His *Confession* seems to be written as an old man who shares his honest struggles without triumphant accomplishments. He seems to be defending himself from the betrayal of a confidant and friend who first promoted him for ordination as bishop and then turned on him, divulging a lapse in his early years. This confidant received Patrick's preordination sacrament of penance wherein he spoke of a serious sin that happened in a single hour thirty years prior. This was held against him when he was to be ordained a bishop and sent to Ireland after Palladius in 432 CE. His *Letter to the Soldiers of Coroticus* is an anguished cry of grief after newly baptized young Christians were imprisoned, enslaved, sold, battered, and then murdered. There's no historical evidence that Patrick was given great adulation during his lifetime.

It is after his death that other writings were attributed to him, including *The Lorica of St. Patrick* and *The Hymn of Secundinus*. Legends abound about banishing snakes, using the three-leaf clover for a symbol of Trinity, lighting the Easter fire, healing, consoling, and encouraging the full sacramental enfolding of Christian membership. His legacy can be trusted; it seems to me that Patrick's suffering produced great holiness for all of us descendants of the Irish Catholic Church. His genius seems to be that his suffering as a boy, an ordained priest, and then a bishop was fuel for his faith. He trusted, he prayed, he believed, and he taught the *kerygma* that was dear to his heart. The teachings were no mere apologetic rhetoric learned at some council or in some debate on a veranda of some Italian villa. His faith was rendered from nights on cold, damp Irish mountains herding the swine for his master. His suffering gave him empathy for the Irish people. He shared the new faith rather than dominating and obliterating the old customs and beliefs.

Patrick used his training period to learn from the people he lived with: he knew from immersion the ways of the Druids. He used intelligence, not might, to conquer the Irish. Since he was not trained in Rome for a classical liberal education, he was simply sharing the essentials of the faith from his consciousness of Christ in Trinity. He shared his own faith, his own spirit-filled energies, his own immersion into the light of mysticism.

What did he learn while being a slave? He did not return as a warrior or a political arm of the Roman Church but as a bishop who offered the Christian way of life: the Good News (*kerygma*), community (*koinōnia*), liturgy (*leitourgia*), and service (*diakōnia*). Missing was power and control of a new system from afar. The Druids taught him mysticism. He taught the Druids a personal Christ who would give each distinct soul a life after this one on earth.

Not unlike the new physics of today, the Druids viewed the world in a way that we might call miasmic, like the turf in Ireland. The illusion we have of things being discrete, of objects and people having a material (call it "existential metaphysics") integrity—that things and people stand alone and unconnected—is just that: an illusion. The fact is that everything in the world weaves into everything else and melds into existence, like the roots of a tree digging into and becoming enmeshed in the earth. This could not have been more different from the way that people in other parts of the world, like the coast of Turkey or France, approached the relationships among people, creation, and material objects. While the

Greeks were impressed with the crystalline separate-
ness of everything and how clearly objects stood out in
the Aegean or Mediterranean sunlight, the Druids saw
a vaporous mist of everything, permeating everything
else; even thoughts wove in and out of people, as well
as nature, like wispy tendrils of a rolling fog.

The wisdom developed by the Druids maintained
the reality of what we know to be true: everything is
connected to its surroundings. Things flow into things,
thoughts into thought, people into the earth and back
again. The system that would derive from this approach
would be open and pluralistic, receptive of wisdom or
insight from wherever it came. Celtic wisdom would see
the person as not quite a separate entity but inured into
an earthly ground of existence.[16]

The Druids developed this approach into a complete
system of rituals. Patrick recognized truth wherever
he found it. Then, he used his personal influence: he
befriended a chief, a woman in need, a sick child, and
people here and there. He attracted a crowd but was
attentive to the person before him. The particularity of
the human Jesus being the Christ of the Cosmos was a
perfect fit for the Irish intellect. The wisdom of the Druids—to name the undifferentiated matter that we call
mystery—was appropriated by Patrick since he had his
own experience of the presence of Trinity: Father, Son,
and Holy Spirit. Again, the exchange was sweet: Patrick
learned the ways of mystery and consciousness through
the Celtic spirituality. Then he proclaimed the Good News

that all were saved and would have life in Christ during this lifetime and in the next.

The Christ consciousness prayer[17] attributed to the spirit of St. Patrick is a masterpiece that inspires and transmits the practice of a morning offering by a an awake Christian:

> Christ with me,
> Christ before me,
> Christ behind me,
> Christ in me,
> Christ beneath me,
> Christ above me,
> Christ on my right,
> Christ on my left,
> Christ when I lie down,
> Christ when I sit down,
> Christ when I arise,
> Christ in the heart of every man
> who thinks of me,
> Christ in the mouth of everyone
> who speaks of me,
> Christ in every eye
> that sees me,
> Christ in every ear
> that hears me.[18]

St. Benedict and St. Patrick offer examples of how discernment is the method of using prayer and life experience to walk toward, with, and in God. We see that

they had to make difficult choices and take the consequences for listening with the ear of their heart. It is that
same Spirit alive in and around us that urges us to do the
same. We might be called to an invisible path of humble
service in our monastic vocation or we might be inserted
in the public eye like Thomas Merton, but what matters
is hearing and heeding the voice of the Spirit.

Summary and Conclusion

*D*iscernment Matters: Listening with the Ear of the Heart is the fifth book in the Matters Series. The Pentecost experience, in which we acquire the Holy Spirit, is ours if we ask. We must open that door from the inside. God is gentle and respects the autonomy of creatures. The Holy Spirit is the New Covenant, a law engraved in our hearts. When we listen, we hear that distinctive voice that Jesus promised us when he left this earthly realm. The Holy Spirit is the reign of God in our hearts. At first, it is a moral voice, but after some practice, this intuitive grasping and personal relationship springs forth into a mystical dynamic of the human loving the Divine. We listen with the ear of our heart, and, like Moses, we have an inner posture of our shoes off. We feel the warm stirrings of grace to rise. All is sheer grace.

Afterword

We always want God to decide for us. That does not mean that we are always ready to respect God's decisions. In fact, God wants us to make our own decisions and assume full responsibility for them. It is true that the Bible gives the example of some people who were chosen by God to fulfill a special mission for the people of God. Those situations, however, are rare. God expects us to make all the decisions that have to be made in our daily life and throughout our whole existence ourselves.

Before a difficult choice, we easily pray that the Holy Spirit indicate to us what we should do. This form of prayer may be a subtle way of copping out of our responsibility. Yes, we must pray to the Holy Spirit, but what we ought to seek is the purity of heart that will allow us to make the right discernment. Because it is always a question of discernment and not of hearing an outside voice that will tell me what to do and will dispense me from the difficult responsibility of making a decision and accepting the responsibility for it.

Suppose I have to take part in an abbatial election. Should I pray that the name of God's candidate be revealed to me? No. God has no candidate. In God's plan, the electors have the full responsibility of choosing one of them as Christ's representative in their midst. The one they will choose will become God's candidate. What a responsibility they have! They certainly ought to pray to the Holy Spirit, asking for a pure heart, to allow them to see each one of their brothers or sisters with God's eyes and to be as humble and detached as possible in making their decision.

In the life of every person, and therefore also in the life of a Christian and of a monk or nun, there are hundreds of such decisions—some more important, some less—to be made daily. Each time a form of discernment is required.

God's will is not written somewhere up in heaven. It is written in our hearts and in every fiber of our beings. We are born with a lot of gifts that need to be used at the service of our sisters and brothers. To discern those gifts, which are so many graces and calls, is the first form of discernment. Part of the beauty of our nature as created beings is also that we have limitations. To get to know those limitations and how to deal with them is another form of necessary discernment. And we have our sins!

We belong to a society, to a church, to a family, to a community, to many forms of associations. We constantly have to make decisions concerning the way to be at the service of others while respecting other persons' gifts and limitations as well as our own. This requires discernment.

As Christians, and also as monastics, we belong to a long tradition. In it, we have a long series of witnesses, of wise and holy men and women who not only constantly made the right discernments but developed tools that allowed them to make the right choices.

Cassian was a great knower of the human heart. He has two conferences on prayer that are among the most beautiful texts written on the subject. And most of what he has to say about it is how to let our hearts be cleaned so that the right choices will be done and prayer will happen. This is what discernment is all about.

We must be grateful to Sister Meg Funk to have condensed in a few pages so many of the tools developed by women and men of God throughout the centuries to make adequate discernments.

This is not leaving the Holy Spirit aside. The Spirit is within our hearts. The process of discernment is a process of purification that allows us to penetrate deep enough in our hearts so as to become one with the Spirit. To obey is not doing someone else's will; it is to have the same will. And this is the ultimate form of prayer in which, in the words of Paul, our voice and that of the Spirit becomes one single Voice saying *Abba*.

Armand Veilleux, OCSO
Abbot
Abbaye de Scourmont

Notes

Iconographer's Preface

1. "God became human so that human beings may become God" (St. Athanasius). For the Eastern fathers, the formulation of the doctrine of deification affirmed the reality of humanity's innermost hope as "belonging to God." St. Gregory Nazianzus argued that the root of a person's true greatness and calling lay in being "called to be a god." Elsewhere, St. Basil the Great insists that "the goal of our calling is to become like God." The ultimate redemptive destiny of humanity is none other than to attain likeness to God and union with him. Deification denotes a direct union and a total transformation of the human person with the living God by divine grace. St. Basil the Great says that human beings are nothing less than creatures that have received the order to become gods. The descent (*katavasis*) of God has offered the created order the capability of ascending (*anavasis*) to the Divine in the Holy Spirit. For the Eastern fathers, deification is God's greatest gift to, and the innermost goal of, human existence. Although the term does not occur in the Holy Scriptures, the Greek fathers believed that it was a fitting theological term affirming the command of 2 Pet 1:4, that is, "to become participants of the divine nature."

2. See Phil 1:9-10.

3. Literally: "He [God] rested from all his work which God created to do or make" (Gen 2:3b).

4. See Exod 3:7-10.

Introduction

1. See *Thoughts Matter: Discovering the Spiritual Journey*, *Tools Matter: Beginning the Spiritual Journey*, *Humility Matters: Toward Purity of Heart*, and *Lectio Matters: Before the Burning Bush*, all published by Liturgical Press in 2013.

2. *Lectio divina* is a way of praying using the revelatory texts of Scripture, nature, or experience. This encounter with God is to listen with the ear of your heart. *Lectio divina* is our burning bush. We take off our sandals and bow our brow to the ground of our being. We invoke the Holy Spirit to bring to mind our particular text to use for *lectio divina* in the coming months. We linger with this text for months or until another text rises from underneath our consciousness.

We listen to the literal voice and study with our logical minds. We meditate on the symbolic voice with our intuitive minds. We heed the moral voice with our personal senses of prayer and ascetical practices. We live the inner voice through our daily decisions and through the discipline of discernment. We receive the mystical voice with our spiritual senses.

Each of these voices is distinct and is mediated through the revelatory text. Our part in this encounter is to listen, meditate, heed with discrimination, and receive. This way of personal prayer becomes our way of life, a culture of God consciousness. This method depends on the Holy Spirit enlightening our minds and filling our hearts with desire. The text is given to us as individuals, and we all take the necessary days, weeks, and months to live into the revelation. This is sustained *lectio*. *Lectio divina* is an encounter with the living God within our loving hearts. This is our individual practice that prepares us for liturgy, selfless service, community life, friendships, and an ecclesial way of being in the world.

Skills of study, artistic appreciation, training of the mind for discipline, and a disposition of repentance prepare us for the deepest experience of the revelation of God. Discernment, listening with the ear of the heart, becomes a way of life.

3. See my *Lectio Matters*, xxv–xxxv.

4. Yves Congar, *I Believe in the Holy Spirit* (New York: Crossroad, 1997). This eight-hundred-page book is a comprehensive study of the Holy Spirit in the Roman Catholic Church that gives the background for Vatican II and its restoration of a theology of the Holy Spirit (*pneumatology*).

5. Stanley M. Burgess, *The Holy Spirit: Eastern Christian Traditions* (Peabody, MA: Hendrickson Publishers, 1997). The Christian West has much to learn from the Christian East. One should pray for the Holy Spirit to come. One should renounce sin and be ready for this New Life that is actually our original baptismal life in Christ Jesus. There are no limitations to where, how, to whom, how deep, and how pervasive is the Holy Spirit.

6. I can distinctly remember when I realized this for myself. It was about twenty years ago. I was teaching in room 108 at Benedict Inn and putting on the chalkboard a primitive drawing of how Jesus being human and God linked us to the Three Persons in One God. It was so simple. I got it!

7. John Cassian (366–430) took two seven-year journeys with his older friend, Germanus. They traveled from Rome to Egypt, Palestine, and Syria. John Cassian founded two monasteries in today's southern France. The pilgrimage was a sacred journey to meet the desert fathers and mothers. They lived in those monastic settings and listened to their teachings. Cassian wrote *The Conferences* (trans. Boniface Ramsey, Ancient Christian Writers 57 [New York: Newman / Paulist Press, 1997]) and *The Institutes* (trans. Boniface Ramsey,

Ancient Christian Writers 58 [New York: Newman / Paulist Press, 2000]). Again, these writings are considered the richest and most comprehensive source of the theory of religious life for both Eastern and Western Christianity. Cassian begins this teaching by identifying the afflictions that impede our progress on the spiritual journey.

The end or aim of the spiritual life is union with God, yet before this total union in our next life, we can obtain purity of heart. This proximate goal is to obtain equanimity during our earthly life. This makes possible the experience of contemplating God because a pure heart is free of obstacles that veil the immediacy of God's presence. Our ultimate goal is God.

Chapter 1

1. Catherine Mowry LaCugna, *God for Us: The Trinity and Christian Life* (New York: HarperCollins, 1992). This book of 434 pages is the most intelligent book I have ever read on the Trinity. This is my summary of her main point: The Holy Spirit is the how, the by which, the dynamic force, the personal connection that is given to us through Jesus and because of the Father. The good news is that the Holy Spirit is a Person and is personal like us. The Trinity is an essential relationship that exemplifies what it means to be human. The Christian revelation of God is stunning for its intimacy and personal engagement with me as an individual and with all of us as church. I am quite aware that there are other traditions within our Catholic Church that explicate Trinity as nonpersonal, or impersonal, to offset a tendency to limit the Trinity as a mirror image of God's creatures. In the book *Lectio Matters* I take care to separate the voice of a revelatory text from the senses of the reader. This also helps to prevent a projection of creatures back to Creator that inverts the truth so that each of the three persons of the Blessed Trinity would be like three persons like us who are precipitants of the mystery. While the word person is ambiguous I wanted to show in this book

that God is for us. Therefore, I enjoyed Catherine Maory LaCugna's book that demonstrates that we have a most intimate personal relationship with God who is also personal toward us.

2. Anthony D. Rich, *Discernment in the Desert Fathers:* Diakrisis *in the Life and Thought of Early Egyptian Monasticism* (Carlisle, UK: Paternoster Press, 2007). This is an Oxford doctoral dissertation under Benedicta Ward. It is a comprehensive study with brilliant insights into the literature on discernment in the monastic tradition.

3. William Harmless, *Desert Christians: An Introduction to the Literature of Early Monasticism* (New York: Oxford University Press, 2004). I know of no better book on the literature of the desert tradition. It took me twenty years to thread my way through these sources that St. Benedict used in writing his Rule that we follow today.

4. John Cassian, "Second Conference: On Discretion," in *The Conferences*, trans. Boniface Ramsey, Ancient Christian Writers 57 (Mahwah, NJ: Newman / Paulist Press, 1997), 99: "With every effort, then, the good of discretion must be acquired by the virtue of humility, which can keep both extremes from hurting us. It is an old saying that extremes meet. . . . For the extreme of fasting comes to the same end as overeating does, and the excessive prolongation of a vigil is as detrimental to a monk as the torpor of a heavy sleep is" (2.16.1). It's equally adverse to have too little as too much of a thing.

5. See Irénée Hausherr, *Spiritual Direction in the Early Christian East*, Cistercian Studies Series 116 (Kalamazoo, MI: Cistercian Publications, 1990), 157.

6. John Climacus, *The Ladder of Divine Ascent*, trans. Colm Luibheid and Norman Russell (New York: Paulist Press, 1982), 62.

7. See John Cassian, *The Institutes*, trans. Boniface Ramsey, Ancient Christian Writers 58 (Mahwah, NJ: Newman / Paulist Press, 2000).

8. Kathleen Cahalan, *Introducing the Practice of Ministry* (Collegeville, MN: Liturgical Press, 2010). Cahalan is an original thinker

with a researcher's gift for depth and breadth. Her writing makes a compelling case that ministry is the practice of the Trinity. I recommend this book to people who come to me and are discerning their ministry. I also recommend this book of Dr. Cahalan for those who find the personal tradition of the Trinity to be obscured by too many images. In this book the concept of the Trinity is not the point. We can have our own experience of Trinity through practice. Trinity is an economy of relationship that takes the whole of us and all our parts. This mystery is only grasped by doing it.

9. Katherine Howard, *Praying with Benedict* (Winona, MN: St. Mary's Press, 1996), 81.

Chapter 2

1. Evagrius of Pontus, *Talking Back (*Antirrhetikos*): A Monastic Handbook for Combating Demons*, trans. David Brakke, Cistercian Studies Series 229 (Collegeville, MN: Liturgical Press, 2009).

2. Fr. Daniel Chowning, a Carmelite priest who has done much study and teaching about prayer, shared the latest discovery about the original writing of this practice:

> I recently ordered from France the new edition of *Abandonment to Divine Providence* by Jean-Pierre de Caussade. To my great surprise the latest research has discovered that de Caussade is not the author of *Abandonment to Divine Providence*. The introduction to the new edition, published by *Christus*, a Jesuit publication in France, has a lengthy introduction explaining that the author of *Abandonment* was a disciple of Madame de Guyon. The composition, the themes are reflective of the "Guyonienne" spirituality. The literary style is quite different from de Caussade's letters, which are a mine of spiritual wealth.

> I find this quite interesting. As you may know, Madame Guyon went under scrutiny and was accused of being a "Quietist" along with Fenelon.

3. *The Cloud of Unknowing and the Book of Privy Counseling*, ed. William Johnston (New York: Image Books, 1973).

4. Ibid., 87.

5. Ibid., 153.

6. Teresa of Avila, *The Way of Perfection*, in *The Collected Works of Teresa of Avila*, trans. Kieran Kavanaugh and Otilio Rodriguez, vol. 2 (Washington, DC: ICS Publications, 1980), 140.

7. Ibid., 147.

8. Ibid., 133.

9. Ibid., 128–48.

10. Ibid., 149.

11. Teresa of Avila, *The Interior Castle*, in *The Collected Works*, vol. 2, 270ff.

12. Gabrielle Bossis, *He and I*, trans. Evelyn M. Brown (Sherbrooke, QC, Canada: Éditions Médiaspaul, 1998). Originally published as *Lui Et Moi* by Beauchesne et ses Fils, 117 rue de Rennes, Paris, 1969.

13. St. Isaiah the Solitary, "On Guarding the Intellect," in *The Philokalia*, ed. G. E. H. Palmer, Philip Sherrard, and Kallistos Ware, vol. 1 (London: Faber and Faber, 1979). The hesychast tradition understands repentance to involve guarding the heart: "Be attentive to yourself, so that nothing destructive can separate you from the love of God. Guard your heart, and do not grow listless and say: 'How shall I guard it since I am a sinner?' For when a man abandons his sins and returns to God, his repentance regenerates him and renews him entirely" (26).

Chapter 3

1. See Nil Sorsky, *Nil Sorsky: The Complete Writings*, ed. and trans. George A. Maloney (New York: Paulist Press, 2003); George A. Maloney, *Russian Hesychasm: The Spirituality of Nil Sorskij* (The Hague: Mouton, 1973); http://www.hermitary.com/articles/nil_sorsky.

html; Nil Sorsky, *Nil Sorsky: The Authentic Writings*, trans. David M. Goldrank, Cistercian Studies Series 221 (Kalamazoo, MI: Cistercian Publication, 2008).

2. Sorsky, *The Complete Writings*, 78.

3. Ibid., 79.

4. Ibid., 80.

5. Ibid., 83.

Chapter 4

1. St. Enda: A few years before the historical St. Benedict came from Rome to Monte Cassino, there was an Irish abbot who, after making several monastic foundations on Ireland, established a monastery on the island of Inishmore (Aran Island near Galway). This foundation was famous for training other founders of monasteries that dominated that part of the world for over one thousand years. St. Enda was a near contemporary of St. Patrick, living around 480, the same year attributed to the birth of St. Benedict. St. Enda established the whole island of Inishmore to be a monastic settlement, famous in his day like Mount Athos is known today.

2. Irenee Hausherr, Penthos*: The Doctrine of Compunction in the Christian East*, Cistercian Studies Series 53 (Kalamazoo, MI: Cistercian Publications, 1982), 71.

Chapter 5

1. Gregory the Great, *Life and Miracles of St. Benedict: Book Two of the* Dialogues, trans. Odo J. Zimmermann and Benedict R. Avery (Collegeville, MN: Liturgical Press, 1949).

2. Ibid., 2.

3. Ibid., 11.

4. Ibid.

5. Ibid., 40.

6. Terrence G. Kardong, "Installation of the Abbot," in *Benedict's Rule: A Translation and Commentary* (Collegeville, MN: Liturgical Press, 1996), 526ff. To appreciate Benedict's insistence on discretion, see chapter 64, "The Installation of the Abbot."

7. Greg Tobin, *The Wisdom of St. Patrick* (New York: The Fall River Press, 2004), 43.

8. Quotation in Yves Congar, *I Believe in the Holy Spirit*, trans. David Smith (New York: Crossroad Herder, 1983), 70.

9. Ibid.

10. P.A.O. Siochain, *Aran: Islands of Legend*, 4th ed. (Dubhlinn, Ireland: Kells Publishing Co. Ltd., 1990), 64.

11. Tobin, *The Wisdom of St. Patrick*, 202.

12. Ibid.

13. Ibid., 203.

14. Ibid., 205.

15. Ibid., 67.

16. Tobin, *The Wisdom of St. Patrick*, 93.

17. This prayer is often called "St. Patrick's Breastplate" because of those parts that seek God's protection. It is also sometimes called "The Deer's Cry" or "The Lorica." The whole prayer is stunning! As Dr. Catherine Hindle of Wales has written to me, "The beauty of his morning offering for me is that it begins with everything around me—I arise today through . . . light of sun, radiance of moon, splendor of fire, speed of lightning, swiftness of wind, etc., but leads on to I arise today with . . . God's strength . . . God's shield . . . God's way . . . until all is caught up into Christ—with me, before me, behind me, in me, in others, etc."

18. Tobin, *The Wisdom of St. Patrick*, 230–31.

Resources for Discernment

Please see my current website: http://megfunk.com/
and the original site: http://megfunk.com/old/